Jon.

Hey man I hope this gives you a few laughs. Relax its FICTION! Ha Ha

All the Best.

[signature]

THE GREAT AMERICAN
STAY-AT-HOME-WIVES
CONSPIRACY

THE GREAT AMERICAN STAY-AT-HOME-WIVES CONSPIRACY

Dan Merchant
B. Scott Taylor

TAOW Books

FIRST EDITION

Designed by Blackfish Creative.
Cover Photography & Author Portraits by Greg Kozawa.

ISBN 0-9755519-0-6

TABLE OF CONTENTS

September 6, 2003

Dear New York Times Editor,

Who am I? It doesn't matter. I am just a man, a husband, a father. A man who knows things he was not meant to know. A man who has seen things he was not meant to see. A man who understands things he was not meant to understand.

What you are about to read may bend your mind. It will contradict things you have believed as true your entire life, but I swear to God in heaven that it's the truth. I will be presenting startling facts and evidence that take up where other explanations leave off. Prepare yourself. My hope is that once you understand what is really going on around you, everyday, when you have the facts about why things happen the way they do, that you will be able to fight back. Boys, we're four touchdowns behind at the two minute warning and we didn't even know we were playing a game.

I never suspected that a conspiracy of global proportions was at work, let alone at work in my own neighborhood...on my street...in my marital bed. I have been living in denial, we all have. Can I turn a blind eye? No. The monster is out of the box, it isn't going back in. I can't just sit here and ignore it, hell no. So despite the great personal risk to myself, I began a treacherous journey deep into the underground world of the stay at home wife. Deceit, propaganda and cunning met me at every turn but I felt it was my duty as an American husband, father and veteran to press on without regard to my personal safety or my sex life.

1

I know I am not the only man to take this journey and I want to acknowledge the brave men who fell before me. Men whose lives have become a sexless blur of "honey do" lists, chick flicks and burgers without buns. Without witnessing their pain and sacrifice I wouldn't have the courage to write the very words you are reading. I write these words with the hope that men of courage will read them and band together to salvage our own lives and, somehow, save our sons from this dark and hideous fate.

Sincerely,

A Friend

July 28, 2003

This is what I remember about my first day of retirement. I've worked hard to reach this day and want to keep a record of my thoughts. Was the work worth it? What have I learned in my life? Am I really such a blowhard that I think the deep thoughts in my journal deserve to be published? My wife Alicia thinks my success story could be an inspiration to underachievers everywhere. Or should that be overachievers? If this pile of shit ever reaches the bookshelves of America it will be because some editor fixed it all anyway. Hell, if Jim "I want to be reincarnated as a women's bicycle seat" McMahon can write his stories down, so can I, right?

"You need anything?" she asked.

The question was simple enough, most people need something, right? I'm sure there have been many times in my 38 years when I would have given a laundry list of things I need. But today I didn't have a quick answer. I don't know about you but I've always been pretty good at being objective about my situation, when I'm up I know it and when I'm down I know it. Today I'm up and not feeling too needy.

Do I need anything? I'm poolside, basking in the summer sun and the equally hot afterglow of selling my Internet company, BrownBox.com to VirtualRelocation.com. Cardboard boxes, pretty glamorous way to get rich, huh? It's funny though, the only thing I hated more than technology was trying to find cardboard boxes whenever I moved. Growing up we were always moving from one apartment to the next. My most vivid childhood memory is carrying a disintegrating box up to the third floor, legs burning as I raced up the stairs, scrambling in vain to reach the landing before the box exploded. Two steps from the landing the bottom gave out and I watched helplessly as six years of Sports Illustrated magazines skated down the staircase. That sucked ass, let me tell you. We're talking about some classic issues too – Ali vs. Frazier I and II, The Dolphins beat the Vikings to go 17-0 and who can forget Cheryl Tiegs' "I didn't think you'd be able to see my nipples through this wet mesh swimsuit" cover. That issue was the big thrill of my young life. Now they were lost, another senseless tragedy that could have been prevented by using a reinforced corrugated cardboard moving box.

In college I was forever helping my buddies move. Usually we'd end up using garbage bags to pack clothes because we could never find enough cardboard moving boxes. Then after college, the moving continued, whether it be the apartment shuffle or helping move some hot babe from the office in the hopes she'd be so grateful that you'd get to help her break in her new digs, if you know what I mean. Now, while I never scored after helping move a hottie, I still maintain the theory is sound. Nobody likes to move so everyone is grateful for your help. You get to be manly by organizing and lifting heavy things and you get to show your sensitive side by not breaking any of her fragile girly stuff, yep, moving is the perfect showcase for a guy. One thing I learned from all that – you can never have enough high quality, corrugated cardboard boxes, am I right? May sound stupid, but if you're the guy who

4

shows up on moving day with two dozen high quality, corrugated cardboard boxes, you get cheered like the guy who shows up at a party with "the extra keg."

So I got a couple of Cal Tech geeks, who spent most of their time in the garage playing Doom, to write a program, we put up a website and it turns out the relocation business on the Internet is big doings. Deep down, I have to believe, I not only helped people with their moving needs, I got a lot of guys laid too.

"Do you need anything?" she repeated.

Do I need anything? People will usually answer that they need money and I understand why. Money can be a pressure point with a spouse. Guys, by their very nature, freak if they can't provide for their families. We'll feel guilty about it and even end up resenting the family that we're busting our hump for. You want to meet an uptight dude, find one who can't support his family. But if you have money, that covers up a lot of other needs. As for me, I now have more money than I could ever spend. I could fill three incinerator barrels full of cash every hour on the hour and it would take decades to burn through all my dough. Of course, if my wife starts two fisting it with the credit cards she might blow it all before I'm worm food, but I doubt it.

Really, the money is great because it buys freedom. I don't have to go anywhere or do anything. There are no money hassles. There are no bosses. There are no more eighteen hour work days. I'm going to spend the rest of my days doing whatever the fuck I want until I'm too old to do it anymore. How many guys have it all? Can you have it all? If you can I might be that guy. I have a beautiful family, a loving wife, four wonderful children…and, like I said, a shit load of money.

"Mike, you're killing me here, do you need anything, a lemonade or something?" Alicia stood over me, eclipsing the blinding sun, her blondish hair catching the light like Meg Ryan in one of her cheesy movies.

I squinted up at her, "Nah, I'm good."

"Okay, fine," she shook her head with a smile, "You'd think I was asking 'what's the meaning of life'?"

I guess when you have time to burn you have the luxury to contemplate every question like it's a deep, meaningful one. No wonder those brainiacs locked up in ivy covered colleges are always writing papers and books about "deep things" – they have nothing else to do. I mean, after they whack off three or four times, what's left to do with the day but deep thinking?

She stepped back and the sun blasted me in the face. "After MAC Snacks we're going down to the indoor pool, the kids think this one's too cold. You going to be alright?"

"Yeah," I said, ignoring my stinging retinas.

"You have plenty of sun screen on?" she asked.

"Yeah."

I could get used to this, chilling out by the pool, working on my George Hamilton tan, writing my memoirs. I've never written anything before, but I feel very important, very literary, think I'll knock off for the day while I'm ahead.

Retirement is going more smoothly than I expected. I thought it would feel like a vacation, the kind where you get jittery after a couple of days because you realize how far behind you're going to be when you have to go back to work. I don't think I'll ever get tired of sitting on my ass in the sun.

July 29, 2003

More pool time. Stick with what works for you, I always say, and when the sun shines in Oregon, don't waste it. I could get used to this gig. I spent three hours comatose in the sun and it feels like I've been sleeping under a burger lamp or something. I don't hear the kids anymore. Alicia's probably taken them to rape and pillage the snack shop or run wild in the gym. I lift my sweaty, one hundred pound head up off the lounge chair and have a look around. I notice two things: the smell of my own sun-burned flesh has a sweet, slightly sickening, coconut smell to it and, I'm the only guy on this crowded sun deck. This is kind of funny because the Multnomah Athletic Club, the oldest club in Portland, used to be a "men only" type deal. The women could hardly go any place but the ladies room. No women in the weight room, no babes in the Men's Bar (that's why they called it the Men's Bar, clever bastards), I'll bet the girls even needed a note from a man to get into the ladies can. I'm not saying that was the right way to do it, although the whole "He Man Woman Hater's Club" thing has a rich tradition, it's just odd to be at the MAC and be the only guy in sight. But as I scan the pool deck I quickly realize this is not a bad thing – look at all the babes. I'm not talking about tight, skinny, clueless teens, I'm talking about one impressive bunch of thirty and forty something wives and mothers. I'm talking about women of experience who have steadfastly refused to let the march of time overtake them. They wear splashy, designer swimsuits. Their hair styles are thoughtful and complement the shape of their face and complexion. Their make-up is simple and tasteful. At a glance, every single one of them is hot in their own way. You should see the curves, majestically enhanced racks everywhere. There must be thirty-three fake breasts out here. By making a distinction between fake and real breasts, I'm not condemning here, merely observing, all right? I don't think guys care if they're fake, a shapely hooter is a shapely hooter, period. Am I right? We still stare at 'em. Sure, I'm a purist, a breast expert since age thirteen, I'll admit the natural breast is superior. I appreciate the battle between gravity and the curve of the bosom as God created it. I mean, there is something magical about the sway when a chick plays beach volleyball or runs in slow motion on the beach. But here's the thing with fake boobs, if they are big enough, they flat out intimidate – everyone is mesmerized by a tiny babe with huge hooters, I've even seen my wife staring. And the guys, forget about it, we're powerless, hypnotized, our minds are wiped blank. We know they're fake, but if they're big enough, those fake boobs have their own gravitational center and draw us in somehow. Don't they? So, yeah, we stare. What do you want? We're impressed. But I'm convinced women dig it. What woman doesn't enjoy being admired? Why do you think they spend five, six, ten thousand dollars to inflate their chests three sizes too big? They're begging for the attention. They want us to shout out things like, "Hey baby, nice rack," or "Honey, that's a balcony you can do Shakespeare from." And, if these females are willing to put out that kind of effort for a little attention, who are we to deny them?

*Pssst . . . by now your wife has probably been jacking you up for reading this book . . . flip the dust jacket over, this might help.

Hey, I know it's not too classy to be checking out the other hot moms while my own – and let me be clear here – equally, if not more attractive, wife is off hassling with my wild monkey children. But I contend my awareness of the hot moms is really a caveman/DNA thing at work here – basic instinct, brother. On some primal level my subconscious instinctively defines the sun deck as the extent of the known universe and thus searches for the best potential mate. This is not a "get my rocks off" deal, I think my genetic programming sees me as the only male in this environment, so it is my obligation to spread my man seed in order to keep humanity going. Right? It's a Charlton Heston thing. He was the Omega Man, last man on earth, so he hangs out with the funky hippie chick – after the mutants are wiped out, he's going to get to some serious banging and repopulate the earth. Or in "The Planet of the Apes," what does he do at the end? Heston grabs Nova, the hottest, most fit human on the planet – I mean this chick in her fur mini-skirt was a fucking rocket ship – and rides off to repopulate the planet. Yeah, he gets bummed out when he finds the Statue of Liberty sticking up out of the sand, what with Earth as he knew it being destroyed and all. But I bet my left nut that as soon as Nova whipped out those perfect tits and uttered "Tay-lor," he said, "Fuck it" and got down to the business of restarting the population. One man's Armageddon is another man's Playboy grotto.

So you understand, my instinct is simply scanning my immediate surroundings for the women with the largest, healthiest mammary glands because they are the best potential mothers for my hypothetical sun deck tribe. And, go with me here, my instinct cannot recognize the difference between superior glands and silicone or saline or whatever it is they're stuffing in there. I hope the ladies understand that our rubbernecks are snapping all by themselves – basic instinct.

You think I'm full of crap? Check this: a guy gets on an airplane with one hundred twenty other passengers, within two minutes he's ranked and categorized the women he'd have sex with if the plane starts going down. Somewhere in the back of his mind he is deciding who he is going to drag from the sea onto the beach of the desert island and restart civilization. The stacked flight attendant in first class? The tan brunette in the business suit in 22F? Maybe the blonde coed who stands over you, belly ring in your face, jiggling mercilessly as she struggles to shove her backpack into the overhead baggage compartment? Keep in mind, these aren't conscious, lustful fantasies, just basic instinct coldly doing its thing. That's my theory anyway. Of course, my wife says I'm twisted because my mother only breast fed me for nine days.

My deep thoughts were interrupted by familiar voices: my family descended on me like locusts.

Cassie, six, my youngest and only girl, bounced up, "Daddy I gotta pee."

With her wild blonde hair she looked like a miniature Alicia, even though people say she resembles me. Cassandra Marie is her full name and her arrival was a shocker because I didn't think I knew how to make girls. Alicia was thrilled – she desperately wanted a girl. I was

11

thrilled because in the months leading to Alicia getting knocked up, I had been having the best sex of my life. Of course, at the time, I didn't know she was trying to get knocked up, I thought Alicia was digging my new beard – seriously the woman just couldn't stay off me. Let me tell you, the sex is never as violent and exciting as when your chick is trying to extract the missing ingredients from your loins. Women have their own primal stuff going on, she used me for my man juice.

Now, I love my little peanut Cassie, she's amazing, but she also scares the shit out of me. I was once a little boy, I get that scene, but clearly I don't understand women. I take a backseat to Alicia on Cassie, I simply adore that little thing – it's all I know how to do.

"Daddy, I really gotta go," she hopped around in place.

"Didn't you pee in the pool, princess?" I teased.

"Timmy said it would turn the water purple," she said.

"What I said was, 'the chemicals in the pool will turn your *skin* purple,' " Timmy corrected. "Kinda like when Veruca Salt turns into a blueberry."

"Who?" asked Alicia.

"Veruca Salt, the girl who turns purple and fat in 'Charlie and the Chocolate Factory.' "

"Timmy, it's not polite to call people fat," Alicia whispered.

"But she was. After she ate the gobstopper she got tubby or chunky or obese like that lard-o in the Subway commercials," he rambled.

"I like Jared," Cassie blurted.

Timothy John is eight going on eighty. He loves to argue about everything and thinks he's always right. His young mind is uncluttered and pays attention to stuff that gets past me, so it sorta seems like he does know everything. We have these conversations and I end up saying things like "Yes, okay, fine, but my point was…" or "You're right, bad example, what I'm trying to say is…"

Andy leaps into the fray, "Anyway, the movie's called 'Willie Wonka and the Chocolate Factory.' "

"I was referring to the book which is entitled 'Charlie and the Chocolate Factory' written by Roald Dahl not the Gene Wilder film inspired by the book," Timmy smugly replied.

Andy hit him. Hard.

As my first born, Andrew Michael reminds me daily of my many failings. He constantly shows off my worst traits: he has a big mouth, his temper explodes like a KISS concert and he's not much of a listener. On the plus side he's got personality to burn. I'm convinced God gives you kids so they can throw your faults back in your face… either that or I'm a crappy dad.

Timmy and Andy battle constantly for "know it all" supremacy. Things will get simpler when they're older and can solve problems like men – by pulling out their wangs and measuring them. Whoever has the biggest unit wins the argument – whatever the argument is, simple, right? Anybody who thinks the world isn't one big dick measuring contest isn't paying attention or has a really small dick.

MEN IN A SENATE SUB-COMMITTEE
RESOLVE AN ARGUMENT:

"Mr. Chairman, I have no recollection of trading arms for hostages."

"Colonel North, at this time the committee would like to ask you to whip it out."

"Certainly, Mr. Chairman," Colonel North replied.

"Senator Kennedy will represent this sub-committee. Mr. Kennedy, if you would please."

"Happy to do so," Kennedy replied.

Zip.

Zip.

Their respective "arguments" were unfurled on the evidence table in full view of the gallery.

"Holy shit. Look at the size of that schlong!" gasped the stenographer.

"Well, I think now we understand how you got a hot piece of ass like Fawn Hall to work for you. Colonel North clearly bests the Senator from the great state of Massachusetts by a full three inches and, therefore, could not have traded arms for hostages," said the Chairman.

Senator Kennedy zipped up and approached the bench. The Chairman covered the microphone with his palm and briefly conferred with his colleague. After a moment, he leaned back into the mic, "Colonel North, the Committee would like to know if your spectacular length and enormous girth were in any way aided by the use of special creams or the Penis Patch."

Colonel North leaned into his lawyers for counsel. He nodded several times and returned to the microphone,

"Mr. Chairman, I can neither confirm nor deny the use of the Penis Patch."

While Timothy and Andy slugged it out poolside, Brent, my youngest boy, his saggy swim trunks showing off a healthy four inches of crack, rolls up on Mom, "Could I please have something to drink?" Brent was cool because no matter what hell is breaking loose he just goes with the flow. He's so mellow it's almost like he belongs to some other family.

Alicia mussed his wet head, "Of course, honey."

Cassie began to giggle, "It's warm and tickly."

"Gross," Timmy pointed to the yellow stream seeping out of Cassie's pink swimsuit. The urine flowed down her leg and began to puddle up at her feet. Andy stomped into the puddle, trying to splash piss on Timmy.

"Mom, Andy is being a butthead ass face."

"Timothy John, we don't talk like that."

I propped up on an elbow, trying to exert some authority without exerting any energy, "Ease up man. Don't be hatin'."

Andy and Timmy gaped at me as if I ripped a fart in church.

"Don't be hatin'?" Andy spat with disgust.

"That's sad," Timmy couldn't look me in the eye.

"I thought that's what the Malibu white guy rapper says," I protested.

"B-rad?"

"Jamie Kennedy is cool Dad. You're not."

Okay, fine, I can take a punch, at least the brothers stood united against something – even if it was me they were united against.

Finally, Alicia intervened, "Boys, enough. Get your towels, we're going." After a moment her eyes turned to me, "Are you coming?"

"Uh, you know, I'm working on my memoirs, I have a few more thoughts to jot down," I said, trying to sound writerly. "I'll catch up to you at MAC Snacks."

"Whatever," is what Alicia said, but her glare said, "No, no, don't even think of getting off your ass and help-ing me you lazy bastard. I've been managing this traveling orphanage just fine all these years. No, you sit back and relax, work on that tan. Enjoy your deep thoughts while I descend into the ninth level of hell with your offspring."

"Do you want anything?" she huffed.

I knew better than to take that bait, "No, I'm good." I waved as my darling wife of fourteen years herded our four kids into the club.

Do I want anything? Actually, yeah, now that I think about it, a little fucking peace and quiet would be great. I'm not going to apologize or feel guilty about it either, so kiss it. I don't know if that's what she was doing just now – trying to make me feel guilty – but, hey, I worked hard for this retirement. If I am being a selfish prick, it's because I earned that right. I really don't think I'm being a selfish prick, though, but sometimes I feel like if I'm not distribut-ing food to the impoverished on the banks of the Ganges or raising children, then everyone thinks I must be half-assing it. When does the school year start anyway?

Alicia and the kids disappeared into the club and I went back to checking out the pool deck scene. The hot moms seem to be divided into small clusters of four or five, and, somehow, the clusters seemed part of an organic whole. Occasionally, one chick moves from one group to another, peering over the top of her designer sunglasses to talk intently with another. Then she returns to her original cluster, bringing back precious new information that sets her group a titter. Reminds me of a bee cross-pollinating flowers or something.

Alicia knows most of these women, but they seem almost generic to me – like women you'd see in a tampon commercial. I didn't know any of them by name except for Kristen, my best buddy's wife. She is slender, tan, long blonde hair, sporting new, perfectly enhanced boobs – she sure didn't look like her thirty five or thirty six years. Well, I take that back, she does look mid-thirties, but she makes mid-thirties look fantastic. All the moms did. Like a fine wine and all that shit. When I was a kid, thirty-five was middle aged, hell, thirty-five was old. My mom at thirty-five was more like Carol Brady – a "mom," not a "woman," know what I mean? These chicks sure seemed to be having a good time, sitting and talking all day, everyday. Seriously, they never shut up. Don't they tire of rambling on about recipes, nail polish and shit? I buried my face in a magazine and casually turned my good ear toward the women.

"How was the cruise?" asked the blonde in the purple tank suit.

"You've never seen water so blue," Kristen replied.

"Where was this?" asked the brunette in the neon green bikini.

"The Adriatic."

"Oh my God, I love Latin America," chimed in the busty red head.

"How did you get Larry to take you on such a fabulous cruise?"

"Are you kidding? I let his mother visit for a weekend," Kristen said.

"Wasn't that last April?" asked Neon Green Bikini.

"Yeah, so?"

"Didn't she watch your kids while you two went to Palm Springs?" asked Purple Tank Suit.

"Do you know how much damage she did in two days? I held Larry responsible for his mother, that cost him 20,000 points and he's been digging out of that hole ever since." Kristen shrugged like it was out of her control.

"You got a weekend at a desert spa and a cruise to the Dalmatian coast all from one mom-in-law visit?" marveled Neon Green Bikini. "You ought to hold a seminar."

"You are the Queen," laughed Purple Tank Suit.

Un-freaking-believable. Larry has been putting in sixty-hour weeks and this yenta is yanking him around, bleeding him dry. Sure Larry's mom is no picnic, but is that his fault? And, yeah, Larry is a bit of a chiseler, but who is perfect? She married him. He's the guy she's chosen to spend her life with. She recited vows before God and friends. What's the point of burning him to the ground in front of her friends? Why not cut the dude some slack?

I gotta say I was a little surprised at what I was hearing. I know about girl talk, but I'd never heard women sound so in charge. Is this a new thing or was I clueless when I was a working man? I also gotta say what I was hearing was making me sick. The only reason these women were hanging poolside in the first place is because their husbands are beating their brains out everyday in the worst economy since Hoover was president. Talk about ungrateful, obnoxious and disrespectful.

Tinkle. Clink. Clink.

I looked up to see something silver glimmering in the sunlight.

"Lookie, lookie what I found," Neon Green Bikini was waving car keys.

"No, he didn't," gasped Kristen.

"Damn straight he did," shot back Neon Green Bikini.

"You deserve it girl. With all you put up with," smiled Purple Tank Suit.

With all she puts up with? Yeah, like what? Whatever she "puts up with" couldn't be worth a new car. She has new boobs packed into a three hundred dollar swimsuit, perfect hair, probably a Botox injection or two holding her face in sixteen year old girl symmetry, what more does she need? I couldn't decipher the make or model but the jangling metal sounded to be of the highest quality.

I involuntarily unleashed a disgusted "guffaw" that probably sounded a bit like "bullshit, bullshit." I coughed to cover and ducked behind my wife's Vogue, hoping the women hadn't heard. I held my breath for a moment. The

19

yammering continued. Either they didn't notice me, or, they didn't care that I was eavesdropping.

"That'll teach him to try and put your kids in public school," Kristen sneered.

"That's a 10,000 point blunder right there. Hello?"

"Who does he think he's dealing with?" piped in a busty red head.

"You can pay me now or you can pay me later," laughed Neon Green Bikini.

"Are you kidding? He's paying now and he's paying later." They all cracked up.

Oh yeah, I think you're all real fucking funny. Let me get this straight. Dude wants to keep his kids in public school and Miss Neon Green Bikini wants to put the kids in private school. Okay, fine, I can see arguments for both. Private school offers a better education, but a less diverse cross section of the funky people on this planet. Plus we are talking about grade school here; finger painting is finger painting, right? The public versus private thing also depends where you live, but around here the public schools are going down hard, so I can see Neon Green Bikini's point of view. All right, the guy coughs up ten, fifteen K per kid or whatever and the missus gets her way. End of story, right? Wrong. The Moms R Us contingent seems to be saying that the guy has made a strategic error for daring to offer a differing point of view and ends up having to buy his wife a new car to make amends? Are you shitting me here? Her perfectly shaped new boobs are probably worth a year's tuition. Those puffy collagen lips ought to cover supplies and that taut Botox forehead would cover gas and maintenance for a year on the Mercedes SUV that delivers the children to the private school each morning. Let's prioritize things here honey, you could lay off the cosmetic surgery smorgasbord and help out a little too. But, of course, her man is an endless well spring of financial prosperity. She needs more money? Go ask Hubby (and he better damn well have it). God help him if he doesn't make his bonus or wants to buy some new golf clubs.

I sat back in the lounge chair, stunned. I've heard a lot of bullshit in my life, a lot of people talking a lot of smack, but I've never heard such crass, naked, unadulterated cynicism spewed from the mouths of happy housewives. And these aren't bitter divorcees or something, these are, supposedly, loving wives and mothers. Have I stumbled into some witches' lair? Some alternate universe of evil housewife twins? The math isn't adding up to me at all. Who do these chicks think they are? They sound like plantation owners, sending the slaves into the field and reaping the profits from their labors. And what is with this point thing? Ten thousand points, twenty thousand points? What the hell is that, some kind of housewife rating system?

As I spy on these ungrateful bimbos, I realize they are slacking off big time. Where are all the kids? Who is watching the fucking kids? Most are in the pool, under the care of a bored college-aged lifeguard. What are these women doing to earn their share anyway? Their big effort of the day is to cough up some dough so their little angels can go raise hell at the snack bar. I can see Purple Tank Suit now, "Mommy is talking to Aunt Kristen. Here, honey, have five

21

bucks, buy some candy, let that sugar hit your blood stream like a speedball and then go spread your joy."

I don't want to be a dick here, but it is against House Rules at the club for junior members under eleven to be unsupervised. I'll bet there are a dozen kids playing tag in the new weight room right this minute. And you can't blame the little monkeys, they don't know any better. Life is a playground to any kid. Hell, I'd love to be playing tag in the weight room. But children need parameters. They need boundaries. If they aren't raised up with boundaries they become maniacal little mutant freaks who ransack society just the way they're probably ransacking the Men's Locker Room. Who is to blame? I'll tell you, it's these women who are yacking up a storm on the sun deck instead of setting boundaries for their kids. These are the same women who will complain to their stressed out, over worked husbands that they've "been with the kids" all day. Bullshit. They've been poolside all day, it's the lifeguards who will go home totally spent.

I'm sorry but Kristen's got me just a little pissed off. Larry is a good bud. I've known him for almost twenty years and he's never spoken a bad word to me about his wife – and I'm his best friend. Not only does he keep mum on all the crap, Larry even lies to me about Kristen to make her seem better than she is. He tries to tell me Kristen is smart, funny and a great lover. He literally said to me, "My wife is the best lay I've ever had." Liar. He dated Lisa Caudill in college and Lisa was unbelievable. Lisa coma-tose has more sex appeal than Angelina Jolie in her skin tight "Tomb Raider" gear. Now Kristen is pretty hot, I'll grant you that. But no way is she a better lay than Lisa, no way. Kristen's uptight at her core, she always seems like she's holding something back, like her soul is clenched into a tight little ball. Lisa Caudill let it all flow. She had charisma, this grace, this electricity that moved through her. She made you feel special when she spoke to you, when she turned her green eyes on you. Amazing girl. I know I'll think of her as I lie on my death bed and she wasn't even *my* girlfriend. Once she kissed me on the cheek. It was on graduation day, she kissed my left cheek and gave me a hug that altered my beliefs. Because of Lisa I finally understood all that Helen of Troy, "the face that launched a thousand ships" stuff. I would've done anything for her, but Larry the dumbshit dumped her for Kristen. Kristen is all right, but she's no Lisa Caudill.

So where does Larry get off trying to tell me that his uptight wife of twelve years can hold a candle to the "All Time It Girl"? His dedication is admirable, if misguided. But here's the pisser, how does she return the favor? By mocking and ridiculing Larry in front of twenty fellow cult members? Nice. Larry's nobly holding the party line and Kristen's bragging about working him over for a luxury vacation. In a court of law they'd call that "habeas bullshit."

Crash.

Tiny bits of glass scattered all around my lounge chair. My damn glass of iced tea had slipped through my fingers and now forty eyeballs were glued to me.

"Don't worry, I'm not driving," I forced a laugh.

23

Nothing. Tough room. Only distant splashing and, I swear, tumbleweed rolled past.

As I picked up the glass shards, I sensed a shift in the wind. Maybe the housewives hadn't noticed me before, but they sure did now. So much for the invisible man act. I quickly retreated behind a magazine. A shadow fell across me, I looked up to see a white clad waitress offering me a fresh iced tea. That was fast. She jotted down my member number and disappeared as suddenly as she had appeared.

Casually, I tried to recapture my veil of secrecy by pretending to be immersed in my wife's Vogue magazine. As my ears scanned the sun deck, I thumbed through the glossy pages and was momentarily distracted by an article entitled, "Why Men Like Blow Jobs." A moving, articulate, well written and, dare I say it, challenging piece that every woman in North America should commit to memory. However, history has shown that such riveting journalism rarely influences the readership. Every woman's magazine inevitably publishes similarly important articles and yet, we never see an increase in blow job frequency, on a national level. This is puzzling because every time they put Jennifer Aniston and her new hair cut on the cover they start a sensation. And yet, these same magazines can't manage to turn oral sex into the latest fad among America's housewives. Oh, sure, I've heard the stories about how oral sex is the latest thing in high school. How getting to second base is now getting head. The magazines say that since the whole Clinton/Lewinsky thing cheer-leaders are going down on anything, anytime because "it doesn't really count." This may be true, I don't know, but it sounds like the kind of thing someone would make up to sell magazines and spite men. I think the editors of these rags are tricking men into buying these magazines for their wives by plastering these sex headlines all over the covers. Bastards.

I couldn't hear anything from the house fraus now. I had lost the station. I was picking up static on the dial. The pool moms had seemingly switched frequencies. They spoke in hushed tones, conscious that they were indeed in mixed company. As I strained to listen, the animated voices of the women began to shift and drift. I could follow the rhythms of their conversation, but could no longer make out the individual words. I turned on my side, aiming my good ear at the gaggle of housewives – still nothing. Were they even speaking English? I peeked over the top of the magazine, watching their lips move as they yammered on, but I tell you I couldn't make out a single freaking word. These housewives sounded more like chickens in a coop or crickets. You know what it was like, the Bushmen of the Calamari (or wherever those Bushmen are hanging out these days).

Click. Buzz. Pop. Smack. Chirp.

What the hell are they saying? Are they talking about me now? They sound like the skinny native in "The Gods Must Be Crazy."

Click. Pop. Chirp. Cluck. Smack.

The harder I listened the more alien their language became. Was this some kind of special "Wife Speak"? Some kind of code talk? During World War II the U.S. Army used

Navajo Indians to relay messages so that the Japanese couldn't break our code. But I'm telling you that this wasn't NavaJo or Japanese. Hell, the Enigma code breaker would melt down trying to decipher this mumbo jumbo.

But it seemed more like a language than a code, flowing naturally like conversation. But when would a bunch of housewives have time to create their own language? Dumb question – they have been sitting poolside all summer and when they're not here they're sitting in the Starbucks. So, hypothetically speaking, there was time, plenty of fucking time. But really, why would they bother, everybody knows that men don't listen anyway.

I began to notice a dull ache behind my eyes. Then I started to see stars. The harder I tried to concentrate on the chatter the more dizzy I became. Suddenly, my chin dipped into my chest. My head was bobbing like I was in high school Geometry all over again. I was fighting a losing battle against sleep. A weird numbness overwhelmed my head and I was powerless to block out the voices. Maybe somebody put something in my drink.

Chirp. Chirp. Pop. Cluck. Smack. Click.

Next thing I remember Andy, my twelve year old, is staring down at me.

"Hey, Mom, Dad's got some funky white junk on his lip."

Alicia hovered over me, "How was your nap?"

I rolled over and struggled to sit up, groggy as hell. How long had I been out? What happened to me? What day is it?

"Oh, Mike, the whole side of your face is sun burned. You look like a Maine lobster," Alicia helpfully pointed out. "That must hurt. Didn't you put on the sun block? I left it in the bag for you. Well, nothing to do now but to wait for it to peel off."

I was still regaining consciousness, but I swear the gaggle of housewives was staring at me. Every woman, every little group, sat at attention on their lounge chairs, eyeballing me. It was very creepy. I think they were trying to levitate me or something. Then Neon Green Bikini made some comment to Busty Red, which I'm sure was at my expense, and all the wives erupted with laughter. I could be paranoid, but I swear, out of the corner of my eye, I saw Alicia give them an embarrassed shrug.

July 31, 2003

Alicia's initial support of my memoirs has disintegrated into mockery already. She flips me shit about it every chance she gets. This morning I was sitting at the kitchen table writing my thoughts and every time she passed through she would mumble, "It was a dark and stormy night..." or "Once upon a time there was a boy..." or "Meanwhile, back at the castle...," very funny honey.

Today is the third day of the rest of my life. Weird, this sure doesn't feel like my life. Nowhere to go. Nothing to do. No men around, they're all at work. I'm not going back to the pool; those housewives freaked me out yesterday. Hypnosis may be too strong a word for it but I think maybe those yentas bored me to sleep with their chatter, literally.

So I'm left to wander through this strange world of women and kids, a world where the phone rings all the time but is never for me. My wife is on the thing non-stop, one call buzzes in while she's talking away and she just switches over to the other line. When she finally hangs up I can't resist asking, "Who were you talking to for an hour and a half?"

"I called Janet about car pooling, then Nell beeped in, then Laura and Kristen called after that," she smiled and shrugged. Alicia is famous for saying, "I never get a minute to myself," now I'm thinking, "hang up the damn phone and you'll get about five hours." What has Thomas Edison begat? Begot? What is that word? I wish I was a little more stupid than I am because then I'd be too stupid to know that I'm not all that smart. You know what I'm saying? The people who are real dumb asses don't realize that they're dumb asses and let me tell you, those truly ignorant dumb asses are some happy fucking people.

This journal is actually backfiring. Instead of a place to reflect on my deep thoughts and life triumphs, writing in this stupid journal is constantly reminding me how stupid I actually am. I used to read books, but always skipped over the words I didn't know. Sometimes I'd highlight those words, intending to look them up, my own cheapskate word a day calendar, but I never actually did. Then I'll be watching MSNBC and hear one of the highlighted words, "Damn, there's that word I don't know. Why are they mocking me?"

I stumble aimlessly around my twelve thousand square foot house as if it were a vacation lodge – it doesn't even feel like my house. I've spent more time in this house this week than I have in the past year since. A number of huge rooms are still empty, but my wife is having a ball planning and ordering and buying and reordering and, well, she can have it. She lives for that shit and I'm glad it makes her happy. This big place just doesn't feel like mine yet, that's all. I expect men in suits to arrive at the door and say "okay, joke's over, there's a camera in the toaster and you're on 'This Dumbshit Thought He Was Rich'. What? You really thought you could make a million dollars selling cardboard over the Internet?"

Hey, maybe I am one of those truly fucking ignorant people after all. I suppose I'm living the dream. I worked my butt off for years – first in the employ of idiots, then building a business from an idea I had jotted down on a Denny's napkin then, all of a sudden, payday, they hand me a pile of money, take my company and say, "see ya bub." Yeah, I know I sold the company, but it feels like they took most of me with it. Who am I now? I'm not CEO of BrownBox.com anymore, I'm just some guy looking for a reason to get dressed. All your life they tell you "get a million dollars, get a million dollars" – okay, fucking did that. American dream, check. Now what?

Okay, I don't expect any sympathy here, I'm just telling you where I'm at with it. I don't know, maybe this journal will help me find some purpose in a new path, a new adventure. Reality is my family and I don't have to worry about money, probably never will have to worry again. But that still doesn't help me with what I'm going to do today. People keep telling me to work on my golf game, but everybody knows that will only make you go crazy faster.

Just re-read that last paragraph. What a fucking whiner! They say you're not supposed to re-read passages until a month after you write them, but, cheez, someone please kick my ass.

Don't get me wrong here, being a millionaire isn't all angst and confusion, I will tell you one very cool thing about having a million dollars. Since I was a little boy, I always wanted to own a Porsche. You didn't see many in the heart of New York City, but when you did you'd stop playing and, out of respect, have a moment of silence until the Porsche disappeared from view. For years I lusted after the classic 911, then at some point, thought the 944, with the wide back, was too cool. As the new millennium rolled around, I had a hard on for the C4 Cabriolet. This thing was the shit: triple black titanium interior, 300 plus horse power, Tiptronic transmission, an ear drum shattering Bose sound system, computerized all wheel drive, satellite navigation system – what more could you want? I searched the Internet and found a 2000 model that was in fantastic condition, but an auto dealer in Bellevue, Washington beat me to it. He paid $96,000 for it. Yeah, I know, $96,000 for one car, it's embarrassing, but you have to understand this C4 is not some stupid Hummer loaded with an NBA stoner quality sound system – just a simple, beautiful automobile. But $96,000, for a car, yes, I do realize I could feed a bunch of families for a bunch of years with that much money, but I'm allowing myself this one personal, selfish indulgence. If you could hear this engine you'd understand what I'm talking about. It sings at 110 miles per hour and doesn't start getting squirrely until 140 miles per hour or so, but if you put the top up you're fine. The more I stared at the picture of this car on the Internet the more I wanted it. I decided to go after this auto dealer dude before he screwed up my machine.

So I take the train up to Seattle and cab it over to the dealership. I stroll into this joint wearing tattered sweats, flip-flops and half a Carl's Jr. burger on my face. It takes me about two seconds to spot my car in the showroom. I hover around it in an obvious way, but not a single sales person comes within shouting distance. Not one. Okay, I did look like an overgrown frat boy and I did refuse to remove my shades, but usually these guys take to people on their lot like sharks take to chum. Finally, ignoring the "for display only" sign, I slide over the side and behind the wheel of my C 4…and then the SWAT team descended.

"Sir, I'm afraid you can't sit in the vehicle," sputtered the sales manager. He had a pinched, weathered face and white hair slicked back like Mickey Rourke in "The Year of the Dragon," that underrated cop drama from "Deer Hunter" director Michael Cimino. That white hair looked a little goofy on Mickey Rourke, but I have to give it to this old sales weasel, he was pulling it off.

"This is an awesome car, dude."

Two other salesmen, his back up, waited for Mickey's signal, "Yes, it certainly is," he squeaked through clenched teeth.

"How much is it?" I asked innocently.

"I'm afraid it's not for sale."

I put on my best dumb ass look, you should have seen it I was brilliant. "Huh? What do you mean it's not for sale?"

"If I could ask you –"

This guy was a chiseler, first class, so I figured, why not be a prick and have a little fun with him. "Don't you sell cars here?"

"Yes, of course we do."

"But you don't want to sell *me* a car?"

"No, that's not it at all."

"A guy has to wear a tuxedo in here to get any service? Is that it? A guy can't dress comfortably and get respected?"

"Sir, if I could ask you to step out of the car, please."

I adjusted the seat and the rear view mirror, "How fast does this baby go? I want a car that goes really, really fast." Mickey and his henchmen moved closer. "C'mon, how much do you want for it?"

"Sir, this car belongs to the owner, it's not for sale." he explained.

"Doesn't the owner own all these cars? That's what they do, right?"

Mickey placed a hand on my shoulder, "I need to ask you to get out of the car."

"I don't think you want to do that. You're making me nervous. When I get nervous I piss myself. How would your boss feel about you letting some dude piss all over his personal private car?" Mickey quickly removed his hand from my person and changed his approach.

"We have a lot of cars that go really, really fast. In fact, I picked up a '99 Camry yesterday. Great condition, low miles, mag wheels, very flashy. I'd be happy to take you for a test drive." Mickey walks away hoping that I'll follow. Poor bastard was getting desperate now.

I call after him, 'I've always wanted a Porsche."

"Haven't we all?" Mickey reluctantly returns, his face bunched up like he's jamming a grumpy. "Listen, friend, I mean no disrespect but do you have any idea what a premium automobile like this costs?"

"I know what this car costs. Your boss man paid $96,000 for it."

Mickey gave me a hard look, "Well, very few people qualify for financing on $96,000," he squinted.

"I don't want to finance it."

This caught my pompous jag off friend by surprise. He didn't know what to think as I fished around in the pocket of my sweat pants and pulled out a dog-eared check.

"I'm not trying to juke anybody here. I just want this car, okay? I'm going to write this check out for one hundred and five thousand dollars. You get to tell your boss you turned the car over in less than a week and made a nice little profit to boot. All you have to do is hand me the keys right now."

With hands trembling, Mickey took the check, "Wait here." He disappeared into the back room and reappeared a few moments later with the keys. Two guys emerged from the service department, opened the showroom doors and rolled me out.

"Good day, sir."

Mickey nodded, impressed I think.

Three minutes later I'm screaming down I-5 at ninety miles per hour. All right, fine, it was closer to a hundred ten, er, twenty miles per hour. I hit the Columbia River, which divides Oregon and Washington, a mere ninety minutes and three speeding tickets later. The thousand dollars in fines were worth it – you should've seen the state troopers checking out my wheels – one of 'em asked if he could take it for a test drive.

"Sure," I said. "If I can borrow your service revolver and hunt pheasant." He didn't think that was very funny.

I get home to show my wife and all she says is, "Your mid-life crisis is starting already, huh?" Not fair. I call total bullshit on that. I've wanted a kick ass Porsche since I had the Corgi car miniature 911 when I was a kid, okay? Was I starting my break down when I was eight? Just because a guy buys a Porsche when he's in his late thirties doesn't mean he's having a mid-life crisis. I'm nowhere near mid-life, unless my lovely wife thinks I'm gonna kick at sixty. Yeah, my hair line is starting to ride up and yeah, maybe my gut is bigger than it used to be and maybe I like it when a waitress flirts with me – but none of that has anything to do with my car. I dig the ultimate sports car because I can drive a hundred and forty miles per hour and it looks cooler than shit and everyone who lays eyes on it wishes it was their car. Call me immature or self indulgent, fair enough, but don't call it a sure sign of a mid-life meltdown.

So you see, being a millionaire does have an upside. After busting ass for years, now I'm sitting around bored off my ass, but my ass is in the driver's seat of a Porsche C4 Cabriolet. I'm reminded of the words of the Little Rascals' Stymie, one of the great thinkers of the Twentieth Century, "I don't know where I'm going, but I'm on my way."

August 1, 2003

It's two in the morning and I'm stretched out on "my" couch in "my" TV room. It's really more of a den, but it's the only room in the house I can watch sports instead of Nicktoons or Dr. Phil. Besides, a man needs at least one room to call his own. You should see this couch, I've had it since my senior year in college and it's a classic, I call it the Beast. The Beast is overstuffed, eight feet long and a pain in the butt to move – I had to take the door off my first apartment just to get it inside. Now the Beast is a museum piece, the fabric worn smooth in several spots and each tear and stain tells a sordid story. And, yeah, I guess you'd notice the vague odor of beer emanating from it. But where some people find a whiff of old, flat beer offensive, I think of it like a beer alarm clock. When I plop down to watch Sportscenter and send up that plume of dusty beer smell, I think to myself "Gee, I feel like a beer." If I don't have the good sense to get a beer when I'm watching sports, the Beast reminds me. It's not just a couch it's a complete reminder to drink system.

But the Beast is legendary mostly because I've had a lot of fun on this couch. And by fun, I mean sex, lots and lots of really good, sweaty, too young and stupid to know any better, sex. My wife hates this couch even though most of the sex I had on this couch was had with her. "It's a dirty, filthy couch," she says. But what she means is "I was a dirty, filthy little girl on that couch." Which is probably why I like it. Alicia was a hellcat too, let me tell you. But my wife has nothing to be ashamed of. I try to console her by reminding her that she married me. It's not like she did all those exhaustive, sexual gymnastics with some dork who dumped her and moved on to the next babe in the office. She did it with me so it's all right. I guess I'm also hoping Alicia will catch a whiff of that beer smell and some semi-retired synapses in her brain will fire off and I'll find her upside down and naked on that couch screaming "get me another straight shot! Get me another straight shot!" Yeah, I know, you can never go home...but a guy can dream can't he?

On each of our last two moves she actually tried to bribe the movers into hauling the Beast away. But I called bullshit on that. It's the one piece of furniture that I own. Come to think of it, it's the only piece of furniture that has been in every house we've owned. Every time we buy a new house Alicia explains, in a condescending way, how none of the furniture we own will "go with" the new house.

"Our Santa Fe furnishings will clash with the Craftsman styling of the new house. We're going to need all new furniture," she insists. She'll start going on about this brand or that style and...and...and I get a dull ache behind my eyes and am unable to follow what she's saying. Your wife does this right? I can't be the only guy whose wife hypnotizes him by babbling on about interior design. I never know what she's talking about. I thought Santa Fe was a place in Mexico or something and Craftsman are tools from Sears. I swear to you she's making half of this stuff up, but whatever, if it makes her happy she can go for it. Buying furniture to me is like buying socks: yeah, you need 'em but you don't think about it much. I wish furniture were cheap like socks though. You know what a New England Farm table with pewter trestles costs? Thank God I'm still amortizing my couch. I traded a half rack of beer for the Beast back in 1983. That investment, computed over the past eighteen years, with interest, well, you can do the math, but that couch cost me something like two cents per year. And really, I don't think of it as furniture, the Beast is a monument to the smokin' hot passion that jump started our relationship…and also a monument to my hellacious junior year in college when girls suddenly, and quite surprisingly, found my smart ass motor mouth attractive. I'm pretty sure none of those girls are going to turn up on this couch, naked and upside down, but I do make sure my address is updated in the alumni directory just in case.

Speaking of which, what am I doing on this couch in the middle of the night, alone? I'm trying to figure that out myself. I know I've been locked out of the bedroom again, this happens occasionally, sometimes I even know why. I understand certain behavior will get you locked out of the bedroom. And though my missus keeps me off guard by avoiding hard and fast guidelines, I have identified a series of offenses that will almost always guarantee me a night on the couch.

THINGS THAT WILL GET YOU
A NIGHT ON THE COUCH:

If I was "too friendly" with an attractive hostess while dining out

This despite the fact that my wife chose the restaurant and then begged me to "work it a little" because she wanted to move from a booth in the back to a table by the window. I cried entrapment all the way to the Beast.

If I remembered the name of an old girlfriend too quickly

Or worse yet, likened the physical attributes of said old girlfriend to a supermodel or pop singer. As in, "Norah Jones looks like a girlfriend I had in high school." Or, "You know that Jessica Simpson is a dead ringer for the girl who took me to the Freshman Sadie Hawkins dance…which I'd like to remind you was way before I met you honey."

If I was too slow to compliment my wife on a new outfit or haircut

As you know, this is a tough one. If you're too quick with "Oh, red hair? I really, really like it," then she'll peg you as insincere and you're on the couch anyway. But if you take it too slow and miss the "authenticity window," you're screwed again. If your wife is getting her hair done, pretty much figure you're on the couch that night.

If I yelled at one of the kids because they, let's say, broke the display case to my autographed Joe Montana football

I'd like to point out that the case was high up on a shelf in my den, which is a room the kids are not allowed to enter without my permission (but they did anyway), and I'm not sorry I yelled at the little monkey because now he knows to keep his skinny butt out of Daddy's room.

If I fell asleep at a family dinner while my brother-in-law was pitching me Amway

Seriously, Amway, in 2003, with Costco and the Internet, who do these clowns think they're fooling now? Of course, it was always a dream to one day introduce myself as Mike O'Brien, Double Diamond Direct. This wank should've been straight with me and said "Bro, I got shit canned from Arby's and I need you to float me while they process my application at Wendy's."

If my wife asks me to go by the store to pick up something for dinner and I don't go to "her" store

I say, "But baby, this store was on the way home from the gym."

And she'll say "But that store is so expensive. What? Are we suddenly made of money?" And I'll say, "Yeah, actually we kind of are, since that whole sale of the Internet company thing." And she'll say, "With that kind of attitude God will probably take all this away from us."

If I hire a drinking buddy to be my accountant

Never mind that Brad is summa cum laude from Georgetown, Alicia rants "I know that sleazy accountant is going to run away with all the money." We end up arguing about the moral character of my buddy Brad who does my taxes and doesn't have the guts to steal my money and hide out in a third world country. The key to finding the right accountant to guard your millions? Make sure amoebic dysentery is their greatest fear.

Plant the image of them sitting on a pristine beach with a pile of your money and convulsing from explosive diarrhea. Nobody wants to shit themselves to death in a foreign country.

If I watch a ballgame on TiVo after I already know who wins

My wife will ask, "Is this the Mariners game?"

"Yeah."

"The one against the Yankees?"

"Yeah."

"The one we were listening to in the car for the last three hours?"

"Yep."

"But you already know the final score."

"Yeah."

"Mariners 4, Yankees 3," she says.

"Uh-huh."

"So why are you watching it if you already know who wins?"

"Because Edgar Martinez hits a triple, then steals home to win it."

"So?"

"Honey. Think about that, Edgar hitting a triple? He can barely walk. He must've hit the hell out of the ball to get all the way to third. And then he steals home? Edgar hasn't stolen home since Reagan was in office. That's why I have to watch it."

If I take my twelve year old son to a rated "R" movie without getting written permission from his mother

Come on, lighten up, it was only "Terminator 3," it was a

cartoon. Yeah, they dropped a couple of f-bombs, but nothing Andy didn't hear at recess in public school, before we got his ass out of that hell hole. And besides, the film is a political science primer considering Arnold will probably be Governor of California and, eventually, president someday. I used to think California was really screwed up, but it'd be awesome if they elected the Terminator as governor. I'll bet we don't see any looting and rioting when the Terminator declares martial law. He'd set that straight, walking around with his sawed off shotgun, dropping catch phrases and kicking thug ass.

If my wife has a cold and I give her one of my prescription amoxicillin tablets, forgetting that she's allergic to penicillin and she swells up like a blowfish

Okay, my bad, I totally blanked on the allergy thing. First came the hives, then big red blotches and then she began to inflate. I gotta say, it took all I had to talk to her with a straight face. She looked like Linda Blair, the little girl in "The Exorcist." I wanted to leave her alone, let her get some rest, but the doctor told me to flush her system. The more liquids I could get in her the quicker the poison would be washed from her system. Perfect, I get to nag her for the next six hours.

"Honey, you need to drink some more tea."

"I'm not thirsty. Your mother smokes pole in hell. Let me sleep," she said.

I wanted to point out that my mother was still among the living, but thought better of pointing that out to Alicia.

"You need to flush the medicine out of your system. The doctor wants you drinking sixteen ounces each hour." I cautiously approached the bed.

"Did you put lemons in it?" She's also allergic to lemons – you can see where this is going. Her eyes rolled back into her head.

"No baby, it's fine. I swear it. Just tea, nothing else."

"Are you trying to kill me?" Her puffy face slowly turned to me.

"That's crazy talk. Why on earth would you think that?"

"You want the million dollars in insurance money," she screams.

If your wife has an allergic reaction and you tell her that you carry less life insurance on her than on yourself

"Honey, we're set for life, remember? Beverly Hillbillies loaded, besides, you're only insured for a hundred grand." Oops. That did it. You'd think I would've seen that one coming, wouldn't you? A word to the wise, keep conversations regarding life insurance brief and vague.

"A hundred grand? You cheap son-of-a-bitch!" I swear she began to levitate at this point, "A hundred grand?"

"Honey, calm down. Why throw away all that money on premiums when I'm the one out in the working world?"

"Let's see you try and replace me with a hundred grand. I hope I do die. Then I could look down from my cloud and watch you and your hundred grand suffer without me."

"Hey, come on, you know women live longer than men anyway and I'm insured for two million dollars, if that makes you feel any better."

She settled down a little. "Two million dollars?"

"Yeah. You and the kids will always be taken care of," I assured her.

"Two million dollars? Don't we have a high fucking opinion of ourselves?"

I was shocked, because she never curses, then I swear her head spun around three times. I set down the pitcher of tea and fled to the couch without being told.

Sometimes you have to know when to pull the plug.

If I made a critical comment about one of her friends

This is the one that sent me to the couch tonight, at least I think it's the reason.

I am a little pissed off and tired of writing. Don't feel like hashing out the fight with my wife, going to watch a little Howard Stern before going to bed, er, going to couch. The more I think about it, I've spent a lot of nights sleeping on the couch.

TWENTY REASONS YOU'RE GOING
TO SLEEP ON THE COUCH TONIGHT:

1. She gets to the bedroom first and locked the door on ya.
2. You decide to sleep on the couch just to teach her a lesson (tactical error moron, she'd rather sleep by herself).
3. She heard you and your buddies talking about her sister's ass.
4. She thinks you sided with her mother in an argument.
5. She says you snore too loud (we both know you don't snore).
6. You called from work to see what time dinner is (so you wouldn't be late), but you woke her up from her afternoon nap and now she's cranky.
7. She busts you staring at some hot chick in a perfume ad in one of her magazines.
8. You made a harmless joke about "doing" the nanny. As if.
9. The nanny wears that smoking hot bikini to the pool and your wife catches you staring. Dammit.
10. Your wife catches you gaping at the nanny – again. Moron.
11. Fall asleep watching the Spice Channel, your kids come down to breakfast to see two chicks banging each other.
12. You invite a friend, who has just been paroled, to stay for a few days without checking it out with the missus. Enjoy bunking with the ex-con.
13. Your wife finds glitter on your boxer shorts (I still have no idea how to explain that one).

14. Your wife's hot friend, the one with the new fake boobs, sits next to you at dinner (that's it, dude, tough break).

15. It's the day your wife starts her period.

16. It's a week before your wife starts her period (cheap shot? yeah, maybe, but I'm the one on the fucking couch).

17. Come home from the cigar bar without delousing. You could end up in the garage for this one.

18. Your wife mentions adoption and you suggest a 16-year-old Italian model you met on a recent business trip to Ibiza.

19. Your wife discovers that a $155 charge to your debit card is for a porn site membership, not a Feed the Children sponsorship (you sick bastard, I hope you're happy).

20. Your wife finds out you've been renting a condo down-town for this hot Blazer Dancer you met at the game (Just kidding, you wouldn't be sent to the couch for this one – you'd be crucified upside down).

August 3, 2003

Woke up this morning with this weird feeling that I might be gay. I panicked for about ten minutes, had a cup of coffee, and decided I was straight after all. That was weird. Glad I didn't act on that impulse. I think the events of last night have me a little screwed in the head. Here's what happened:

The evening started off with a nice dinner with the family. The kids all had great table manners, which was cool but out of the ordinary. I have a weird thing about table manners. I have no trouble picking my nose in the car and wiping it under the driver's seat, but if I see someone chew food with their mouth open I go ape shit. Alicia has the little monkeys about as civilized as can be expected, but I still see more than my share of half chewed food. As it turns out the kids were on their best behavior because they wanted to get away for a Play Station 2 tournament at the neighbors. Isn't summer great for the kids? For three months their lives are one big recess. I was fine with that because the house would be empty, just me, Alicia and...the Beast. It was worth a shot. I helped her do the dishes, and a little flirting and smooching made my intentions clear.

"Okay Mr. Man, but not on that filthy couch, you can get that out of your mind right now," she grinned.

Am I that transparent, that easy to read? I guess so, but, hey, I'm not going to quibble over the small stuff. At least we were on the same page, the planets don't line up like this very often. But on the way to the bedroom something funny happened.

"Oh, you know my friend Debra?"

"No, I don't think so," I said. I wasn't really listening to her. Alicia was two steps ahead as we climbed the stairs and, I'm sorry but my wife has a terrific body for a mother of four. I'll bet I could crack an egg on that ass. Maybe she'll let me try.

"Debra. You know, Debra my best friend?" She insisted.

I pretended to remember, "Oh, sure, Debra."

"She was at the pool the other day, she had on that cute green suit?" Alicia prompted again.

The pool? I had almost blocked out the yammering of those ungrateful housewives at the pool. Oh, she means Neon Green Bikini, her name is Debra? "Oh, you mean Debra," I said.

Alicia waited for me to catch up, "She just bought a new Mercedes convertible."

Now I'm with the program. We're talking about the new car Neon Green Bikini fleeced from her hardworking husband.

"She bought it?" I snickered.

"Yeah."

"Don't you mean, her husband bought it for her?" I corrected her with more condescension in my voice than I intended. "But, I'm sure she deserved it," I backpedaled.

Shut up Mike! Why the hell did I say that? My willing wife, ready to rock my world, is leading me to the bedroom and I throw out a cheap shot? What the hell am I doing picking a fight? I never win the fights. Tonight I'm the prohibitive underdog, Vegas has Alicia as a 5 to 1 favorite.

Ladies and gentlemen, in this corner, standing
five foot six, weighing in at a firm and sexy one
hundred and twenty two pounds, from Charlotte,
North Carolina, the Battling Tarheel, Alicia. In
this corner, standing five foot eleven and seven-eighths,
aw, heck, let's call it an even six feet, weighing in
at one hundred eighty eight pounds, which is only
eighteen pounds above his high school weight,
the Manhattan Mauler, Mike O'Brien.

Alicia stopped in her tracks. "Oh, I think she'd saved up her allowance," the sarcasm dripped from her lips.

The fighters tap gloves and come out swinging.

Body blow. Body blow.

"I just meant, I overheard your friends talking at the pool and it sounded more like a gift or something," I said.

Mauler retreats to his corner. Clearly hurt
by the Battling Tarheel's early flurry.

Alicia's eyes narrowed, "Maybe I don't collect a paycheck, but raising your children and running this house is a full time job."

A left hook connects. Followed
by a vicious right cross.

Okay, sex is off, that much is a given. But how did this become personal? How is this suddenly about my wife? We're not even talking about her, we're talking about Neon Green Bikini. That woman is a different housewife altogether.

"Hold on a second babe."

The Manhattan Mauler goes into the Rope-a-Dope,
laying on the ropes baiting his opponent into tiring

herself out. Muhammad Ali pioneered this strategy –
of course, he got hit so damn much he ended up with
Parkinson's, foggy headed and mumbling.

"Don't 'babe' me, you insensitive bastard," she spat.

"Wait. Hang on a minute here. Debra gets a new car and now you're getting mad at me? I'm confused, aren't we happy for Debra? Isn't that the bottom line? Debra and her new car?"

"Your whole arrogant male attitude really lights me up," she pressed.

Uppercut. Uppercut. Body blow.

"My arrogant attitude? You wanna talk about attitude? You should have heard these friends of yours at the pool."

Mauler clenches, pathetically holding on to the Tarheel
in hopes of avoiding a first round knockout.

"These women were not...well, they weren't nice at all," I continued.

Alicia softened a little, "What do you mean?" I should've realized she was luring me in deeper.

"To be honest, it was disgusting. Debra? Your friend with the car was talking like she'd picked the keys off her husband's corpse, like she'd stolen this car from him. She took this gift from her man and turned it into something ugly. You know? And then Kristen started in about her trip." I tried to stop myself.

The Mauler pushes off, he looks strong, he's
got his legs back, ooh, he head butts her. Now
she's mad. That was a strategic error that's
only going to make his beating worse.

Alicia's eyes narrowed, "What about Kristen?"

I tried to retreat, "Nothing, it's not important. Anything good on TV tonight?"

"You can't bring up my best friend like that and then drop it," she protested.

I thought Debra was her best friend. Who is it? Debra or Kristen? You can't have two best friends. They can both be close friends or good friends but they both can't be best friends.

The two fighters circle the ring,
dancing, sizing each other up.

I lowered my voice, trying to sound sober and balanced. "I don't know what it was exactly, honey, they were talking about their husbands like the guys were slabs of beef hanging in a meat locker waiting to be cut into steaks."

She looked at me blankly. I'm not too good with analogies.

"They didn't sound like they loved them. These women talked like their men owed them their paychecks," I said.

The Mauler, boldly, but sadly, moves
inside with a flurry to the body.

"That's ridiculous. Kristen loves Larry and Debra must really love Kurt to put up with all of his shenanigans," she explained.

The powerful housewife easily
deflects the Mauler's punches.

My blood started to tingle a little. Alicia's responses sounded exactly like the housewives by the pool, almost as if they were all going off the same script or something. Creepy.

The Mauler continues to probe, searching
in vain for a weakness. Jab, jab, jab.

"I think maybe Kristen chose that Adriatic cruise because it was the most expensive vacation she could find. It's almost like she's forcing Larry to work harder and harder, like he's paying off a debt to her. What is that about?"

"That's absurd. Kristen's not like that at all, she's always wanted to visit the Dalmatian Coast. She fulfilled a childhood dream with that trip, don't cheapen it by calling it a whim. And besides, you don't know the half of it, all the crap Larry puts her through."

Crunch. A powerful jab catches the Mauler square on
the chin. He is dazed and desperate. With no hope of
winning a decision, he flails wildly for the knockout.

"Hey, I heard her half of the story and she sounded like a greedy bitch on a power trip," I said. "She may be your best friend but she doesn't respect her man and frankly that makes me want to puke." Alicia gaped, her eyes wide.

The Mauler connected, but the
Battling Tarheel refused to go down.

"You and your old boys network have your heads so far up your own asses you don't see the real world. You dick around at the office until you feel like coming home. You go golfing for five hours and call it a 'business meeting'? Real professional Mike, who do you think you're fooling? And hundred dollar Cuban cigars and twenty-dollar Scotches at a "gentlemen's club" are business expenses? I expect the IRS would find that interesting. You men are making up your own rules as you go along and we're supposed to just play along? I don't think so."

Body blow. Body blow. Jab. Jab.

Left, right combination. Right hook.

"And where do you get off pretending that playing Mr. Businessman is somehow more important than raising kids? When you Captains of Industry fall asleep at the wheel, you just file Chapter 11, apologize to the FTC and bail out with a golden parachute. There is no accountability," she continued the pummeling.

Right hook. Uppercut. Uppercut. Left

cross. Body blow. Body blow. The Manhattan

Mauler can't keep his gloves up. He slumps

back into the corner, trying to cover up.

"But if a mom falls asleep at the wheel, what happens? What happens, Mike? I'll tell you what happens, kids turn into illiterate-rapist-killer-advertising copywriters with poor table manners. 'Hi, Mrs. O'Brien, your son wrote a hot new commercial jingle for Prozac and now everyone is hooked on it and, by the way, we found three co-eds in the dumpster behind his apartment.' Don't talk to me about what we have to put up with. We're carrying the weight of the world here, Jack."

The Mauler's knees buckle. His mouth piece flies

across the ring. He falls face first onto the canvas.

At this point, I'm sure I have no fucking clue what she is ranting about. I know she's mad, I know I made her that way, but I'm having a hell of a time following her argument and trust me, I'm trying. Her lips continued to move, but strangely, they seemed to go out of sync. I stared hard at her mouth, but the words seemed to tumble out in a random order. I think she said something derogatory about Charles Manson's deadbeat father and after that I lost focus. Everything went black.

> *Eight, nine, ten. Knockout. The champ is down.*
> *This one is over. He's going to have a hard time*
> *getting a rematch here, this wasn't the kind of*
> *fight the fans are going to pay to see twice.*

Slam. Click.

The door slammed and locked so fast I hardly saw Alicia disappear into the bedroom. I shook myself and tried to understand what was happening. I noticed a dull ache behind my right eye. What is it with women when they get rolling? I listen to her and end up getting mind fucked. Whether she's talking about a grocery list or her niece's boyfriend troubles, Alicia uses about nine hundred words to make a point where I'd use a single sentence. Most women are like this, aren't they? Even when we are actually trying to listen it's impossible to wade through all the words. Alicia went off on this "old boys network" rant and I'm not sure what her point was. If I were to para-phrase her main point it'd be something like "Men suck, women rule." But her argument kept tripping over itself. What do Cuban cigars have to do with anything? Did she intend them as a symbol of man's self-indulgence or was she moaning because she hates the smell and this was as good a time as any to get a dig in. I swear women are so illogical in their communication that they actually cause a short circuit in our brain wiring. I mean, hell, I practically blacked out talking to her. One minute she's yelling, the next minute the door is slamming in my face. It's like I lost a couple of minutes in time. I may have even been probed by aliens, but I can't be sure. It was all eerily familiar, just like when those yentas at the pool put me under – the more I concentrated the dizzier I became. What does this mean? Does this mean that my wife is one of them? No, I choose not to think that. She can't be one of them.

I knocked on the bedroom door, "Honey, come on. You know I don't think you're like those women. I know our relationship isn't some house of cards held together by money. I didn't mean to imply that."

Nothing. Let's try another route.

"And look, I'm sorry if I was unfair to your friends. You're right, I don't know the whole story. I don't live their lives, how can I possibly understand what they go through on a daily basis. And I know how men can be…"

Nothing.

Damn. That bit about "I know how men can be" is usually good for something. She's really pissed this time. But why, exactly? Because her friend got a Mercedes and I made a joke? Or because her friend got a Mercedes and she didn't? That would be a little junior high school, wouldn't it?

I knocked on the door, again, "Alicia, I'm not exactly sure what we're fighting about here. One minute we're going to do the nasty and the next we're fighting over Debra's Mercedes or something…okay, well, I love you."

Nothing.

"I guess I'll go watch some TV, I'll be in the den, if you feel like talking."

I started to walk away, when I heard her voice. Relieved, I returned to the bedroom door, "What did you say baby?"

No response. I listened closer – she was on the phone. No freaking way. I tiptoed to the hall phone and quietly picked it up. Dial tone. She was on her cell phone, crafty woman. Is she narcing me out to Debra or Kristen or both? I know I've only been "retired" for a couple of days, but I'm beginning to feel like I don't belong in my own house. Things ran pretty smoothly when I was traveling twice a week and putting in fifteen hour work days, but it feels like the more I know the less I understand.

Which brings us up to two in the morning, and yes, I know, it's probably a waste of time to try and dissect a fight with your wife and figure out what you should have done differently. But I'm still pretty chafed by the smack those bimbos were talking at the pool and I'm flat out shocked that my wife doesn't seem to understand. As for our fight, here's what I've been able to figure out so far, and none of it is good: Alicia didn't really want to have sex so she started a fight to get out of it. But she could say the fight was my fault and that way she'd get credit for wanting to have sex without actually having sex.

Continuing to replay the events of the evening, I ask myself, "okay, so she weaseled herself into a sex credit, why? Why go to the trouble? Is there a specific goal in mind?" Now, I'm aware that I'm tired, horny and a bit pissed off, but isn't it a little interesting that she brings up the topic of her friend's new Mercedes just as she's about to put her butt up in the air? Cynical you say? Now, I don't think she's like those other house fraus, but I'm confronted with a disturbing fact: the lease on her SUV is up in two months. Was she trying to establish a connection between sex and a new car? She does me a couple times and whispers in my ear the make and model of her new status symbol.

"Oh God Mike, you are a stud. You are an animal – Mercedes 500 SUV."

"Don't stop baby. You are so hot tonight," I'd pant.

"Do it Mike, do it…DVD player, moon roof and heated seats. Spank me now bitch…all wheel drive, fuel injection."

A plan that devious would totally work. Wow, gotta tip my hat to her there fellas. With that kind of focus and determination you could get more than a new car, you could bust a union, pull off a hostile takeover or win a seat in the Senate. Point Alicia.

But I'll tell you what really cheeses me off, if she wants a fucking new car all she has to do is ask for it. I'll give her anything. I worship the ground she walks on. I'd take a bullet for her. If she wants a new car, I'll get her a new car. I'm like her personal fucking genie. She knows that. So what's the deal? She doesn't want to ask for it? She doesn't want to be beholden to me for it? Would she rather take it? Is this some kind of power struggle? Is that what this is about?

This is the problem with writing down your thoughts. Half of 'em look crazy on paper. I'm telling you, Alicia is not like those women at the pool. She's not, I've known her all these years. She's my partner, we're husband and wife. This is not some shallow corporate arrangement.

I sat on the Beast, making myself nuts so I decided, that's it, stop thinking, go to sleep, it'll all be better in the morning. That's when I turned on the television to wind down, put my brain to sleep. I flipped channels for a few minutes and found Howard Stern on E! . Now this fucking guy is a genius. I know that sounds like an exaggeration, I mean, Einstein was a genius, but think about it, Howard sits around his radio studio and uses his slick charm and superior intellect to talk bimbos out of their clothes. After his radio show becomes #1 in practically every market, they make a movie about his life called "Private Parts." It's a pretty funny movie and it stars Howard as Howard. He didn't let the studio tell him "Jim Carey should play you." Then he gets AC/DC to perform and he casts this hot babe to play his wife. Genius, yes? But here's the really crafty part: at the height of his success he gets a new idea: Howard invites cameras into his studio to videotape his radio show and voila, he has a daily television show too. Every morning he's on the radio, every night he's the star of cable TV – all without expending any extra energy. He's still sitting in his chair, talking into his microphone, inter-viewing stars and looking at tits. All he has to do is "be Howard" – that's how to build an empire. That's genius.

Tonight there's this porn star/stripper/actress on the show. Howard has got her describing how she hooked up with a famous movie star that she refuses to name.

"Was it Russell Crowe?" asks Howard.

"Stop it," the porn star/stripper/actress squealed.

"Tom Hanks?" Artie asks.

"Don't say Tom Hanks. Could you picture Tom Hanks all over this sweet thing? No, I don't see Tom Hanks, Sylvester Stallone, maybe. How old is the guy we're talking about?" pushes Howard.

"I can't say," replies the epitome of virtue.

"Come on. You can tell us. It's just us. We won't tell anybody," Howard grins.

The porn star/stripper/actress giggles.

"Name a movie he was in and then we'll guess and that way you didn't give up his name, we figured it out on our own," suggests Gary.

"No, no, that'd be too easy."

"So is he a big, big star?" asks Robin.

"Okay, okay, let's get back to the story. So you go back to your apartment…"

"I didn't catch your address. It's in Manhattan right?" Artie laughs.

"…you make out for a while. Deep French kissing?"

"D-F-K, baby," Artie shouts from off screen.

"I'll bet you're a great kisser, you wanna make out with me?" Howard asks.

"You're making her blush," laughs Robin.

"No, I'm serious," Howard presses on. "My breath isn't that bad, is it? I brushed this morning, I think."

"I wouldn't do it either," Artie says.

"Okay, okay, what happened after the French kissing, did he put his hands on your body?" Count on Howard to keep things on point.

"Yes, he reached under my dress and fondled my breasts," she replied.

"I'd love to fondle that little ass. Turn around. Let us see that cute little ass. Wow. What a perfect ass," Howard drools.

"Can we see your cans?" asks Artie, respectfully.

"A thousand dollars to see those jugs. Gary, we have a thousand dollars for this lovely young lady, right?" Howard asks.

"Yes," Gary confirms.

"A thousand dollars to drop that top."

Judging by the speed at which her top came off, I have to conclude that her halter top has been removed for far less than a thousand dollars.

"Oh my God. They're perfect," gasps Howard. "Look at them. Seriously, those might be the most perfect breasts I ever seen."

"They're the best breasts in this room," said Robin.

"Wanna see my man boobs?" asks Artie.

"Shut up Artie. You're breaking my concentration. You are fabulous sweetheart, seriously."

"Thank you," she says. The porn star/stripper/actress poses awkwardly, but always with a smile.

About this time a thought stirs in my mind, a dirty thought. I got myself all worked up tonight, without any relief, so I figure if I throw down a whack I'll be relaxed enough to fall asleep on my couch. Right about the time Howard reaches out to fondle the porn star/stripper/actresses breasts I begin to pull the pud. I raise the gleaming spire in no time, racing at break neck speed toward the finish line. I'm whacking like a fourteen year old who thinks he's just invented jerking off, trying to finish before Howard goes to commercial break. And even though they've censored out the porn star/stripper/actresses breasts you can still tell they're incredible. Damn. Howard's gawking, I'm gawking, the porn start/stripper/actress is giggling and…and…and, they go to commercial break, unbelievable. What a bummer and just when…but wait, the commercial is for "Girls Gone Wild." Proof of God for all you atheists out there. For anyone who doesn't have basic cable, "Girls Gone Wild" is a video collection of wholesome, American college girls who party at sunny locales and, somehow, lose their clothes.

And fortunately for the task at, uh, hand, no momentum is lost.

That's right honey, uh-huh.

When you stop to think about it, this whole "Girls Gone Wild" phenomenon is quite amazing. Some jackhole is selling a ninety minute videotape where dozens and dozens of "girls next door" types reenact Phoebe Cates' timeless top dropping scene from "Fast Times At Ridgemont High." As if cued by the sight of bare nipples, the Cars' hit "Moving In Stereo" begins to automatically play in my brain.

Are those things real? You gotta be shitting me.

All these girls seem to need is some stranger to point a video camera at them and they start dirty dancing. Don't these girls know that the sleazy fucker with the camera is going to sell their pictures all over the world? Their brothers and fathers and boyfriends are probably watching right now. These girls must be desperate to be famous in that "I almost made it on Joe Millionaire" kind of way. Or they're really drunk.

Almost there. That's right, toss your hair back baby.

"Throw some beads at me and I'll show you what I've got, big boy," teases the Kansas farm girl.

Beads? Honey, you're in South Padre Island, Texas, at Spring Break, you're not at Mardi Gras. Oh, well, let her have her fun and I'll have mine. I'm not really exploiting these stupid, misguided chicks because I'm only watching the commercial, not actually buying the video. I suppose, morally, I should start some kind of petition to protest the mistreatment of these underage women. Well, actually, they're probably eighteen, so there's nothing illegal going on. And, technically, these girls are making their own choices, exercising their own free will. Who am I to intervene?

Shut up asshole, I'm trying to get off here.

"How typical," the sound of Alicia's voice made my blood run cold, my flag was immediately lowered to half-mast.

"I'm upstairs crying my eyes out and you're down here yanking the wiener." She shook her head and walked out of the den.

Perfect, just perfect...and great, now the "Girls Gone Wild" spot is over. Somehow this Juiceman commercial isn't going to do it for me. Funny, in fifteen years of marriage she'd never walked in on me. Well, actually once when I was in the shower she did. But when she saw what I was doing she stepped into the shower, kneeled down, gave me a look that is permanently burned into my skull and...and that weekend we picked out her Lexus SUV. Holy shit. Why didn't I see it before? She does use sex to control me. Is my own wife one of them? Could it be true?

Back up a second, did she say "yanking the wiener?" Yanking my wiener? That's funny. I've never heard it put like that before. It's kind of like a foreigner butchering the American language. Yanking the wiener? I can tell you that one's not part of my lingo.

TOP TWENTY SLANG EXPRESSIONS
FOR MASTURBATION:

1. Jerking Off
2. Beating Off
3. Spanking the Monkey
4. Pulling the Pud
5. Choking the Chicken
6. Whacking the Bishop
7. Stroking the Stiffy
8. Flogging the Porpoise (or Dolphin, either works)
9. Jerking the Beef
10. Strangling the Snake
11. Swinging the Meat Bat
12. Pulling the Python
13. Walking the One Eyed Trouser Snake
14. Chopping the Redwood
15. Raising the Gleaming Spire
16. Saluting the Flag
17. Cranking the Meat Puppet
18. Taunting the Spitting Snake
19. Shooting Pocket Pool
20. Playing the Skin Flute

Oh, wait, that last one is for blow jobs, isn't it? What is number twenty? Now that's gonna bug me...I want to say it's something with "rod" in it. Anyway, those are classics in most circles, if you have a favorite, shout it out. But I promise you it was not "yanking the wiener." Seriously, that was good.

After Alicia stormed out I just sat there, pants around my ankles, laughing. I heard the bedroom door slam in the distance and I laughed even harder. Yanking the wiener? Freaking amateur, I know what you're all about. I'm onto you now.

August 4, 2003

The summer sun was already above Mount Hood when I crept out of the house just before seven. I wanted to be on the offensive today, not reacting to Alicia's clever woman tricks. I knew I'd struck a chord last night by revealing to her what I'd overheard from the house fraus at the pool…and what I'd realized about my own wife. I've been getting played for fifteen years. I know I may be jumping to conclusions, but somehow I know I'm right and I have to prove it to myself.

I left a note that said I had an early tee time at Pumpkin Ridge, that'd cover me for a few hours. I was leaving the house with a mission. For the first time since I retired I was doing something with a purpose. I had never done anything like what I was planning. Oh, sure, there had been many times throughout our relationship when I had surprised my wife with a fancy gift or trip to some exotic place – but that junk had always been motivated by romance. What I was attempting today was much closer to entrapment. I was about to bestow an elaborate gift on my wife for the sole purpose of watching her reaction. Her response would either prove or disprove my fear: last night was merely a scene in her little play, her affection and all that drama was premeditated. She was trying to manipulate me into getting her a new car like the one her friend has. Now you're probably wondering how going ahead and surprising her with said new car will prove anything. I'm not exactly sure, I hatched this little scheme as I was drifting off to sleep. It seemed genius at the time, in a kind of "I'll show her/I have the element of surprise" kind of way. Maybe buying new cars is a symptom of Post Masterbatus Interruptus Stress Syndrome. In the bright light of day the plan seemed flawed, I guess if she doesn't seem surprised then I know she was expecting it. All right, lay off me, it was the only plan I had.

How do you find a car your wife would enjoy tooling around in? Simple, check out the Starbucks and see what her co-conspirators are driving. As I pulled into the Starbucks parking lot to begin car shopping, my C4 Cabriolet was immediately dwarfed by the absurdly huge Hummers, Expeditions and Suburbans. Why do these tiny women drive such monstrous vehicles anyway? I peeked into the spacious cars and, save for a child safety seat, they're empty. No dry cleaning, no bags of groceries, no fifty pound bags of feed, so what gives? Are they saving room for hundred pound drums of Clinique or Estee Lauder?

While we're talking about cars, I thought the new Volkswagens were perfectly fine chick cars. Sporty, cute, quick and you can still fit three or four kids in 'em. Plenty of room for groceries, dry cleaning and Nordstrom bags. When did an eight passenger vehicle become a moral imperative for a housewife with one kid? Meanwhile, I see guys driving around in Cooper Minis pretending to be Euro and all sophisticated. "Hey, baby, oh yeah." You look like Austin Powers in that goofy little go cart, you stupid homo. Trade that in for a Dodge and do your part to restore balance and harmony to the universe.

I strolled into the coffee shop to get a better look at the drivers of these ginourmous machines and sure enough, the usual suspects are hanging out sucking down caffeine. You have your standard cute moms in spandex yoga gear and chicks in tennis skirts and a few MILFs wearing golf slacks and, let me tell you, this place is packed out. My wife could blend into this crowd and I'm sure she'd happily swap her tired Lexus SUV for an H2 or maybe that new Volvo SUV or the omnipresent Mercedes 500 SUV. This is getting too easy. I'm so inside her head and she doesn't even know it. Without a job to distract me 24/7 this playa is now in the game.

I stepped up to the register where a cute, twenty-something barista with a nose ring met me.

"Would you like to try our new Toffee Mocha?" she asked absently.

"Actually, I just want a house coffee."

"One house coffee," she repeated.

As I waited I read the menu: Peppermint Mocha, Pumpkin Mocha, Cocoa Mocha.

"When are you coming out with the Reese's Peanut Butter Cup Mocha? This place is turning into '31 Flavors', you know with the gummy bears and the sprinkles." I'm such a quick wit. The ladies love it.

The barista glared at me, "What are you talking about?" Maybe that nose ring was in too tight.

Another tough room, "Okay, my bad," I leaned in, "But you gotta relax a little, you might want to think about smoking the whole bong before coming into work."

The barista looked up, alarmed. She whispered, "You can smell the weed?"

Alright, I confess, it was a lucky guess. "Uh, no, barely,

really, no one will notice. Besides the coffee smell in here pretty much covers it," I assured her.

She smiled, relieved, "Hey, I didn't mean to bitch your head off, but hassling with these soccer moms every freaking day makes me wiggy. They strut in here like they run the world, like dropping kids off at day care is a big freaking achievement," she shot a fiendish, insincere smile at a nearby soccer mom. "She should try working here full time and going to school full time. And she should try not having her husband pay for every little thing. Freeloader."

"Freeloader?"

"Nothing. I'm sorry. Here's your coffee." She set the steaming cup down in front of me.

"Could I get one of those heat shield-oven mitt things?"

"Sure."

"You think these women are freeloading off their husbands?"

She glanced down at my wedding ring, "You're married, does your wife work?"

"No, she doesn't."

"No offense, but you probably know exactly what I'm talking about. I'm not judging here, I hope it works for you."

The Manager, early forties, big rock on her hand, attractive, looking more like the clientele than the help, emerged from the back.

The barista suddenly blurted out, "One pound of the Kenya breakfast blend? Would you like that ground for a flat bottom automatic?" Her eyes gestured over to the grinder. I played along.

"Uh, yes. Flat bottom would be fine." I followed her, stealing a glance back at the Manager and several of the house fraus who were watching our conversation with keen interest. The barista dumped the coffee beans into the grinder and hit the button. The sound was deafening, but she leaned into my ear and continued, "I shouldn't really talk here. They're watching me."

I peeked back at the freeloaders.

'Don't look. They're watching. Damn Queens of Leisure, it's gone to their heads. As if getting a man, giving him a child or two and then riding the gravy train is a life. Look at the rings on their fingers, look at their cars, it makes me sick, what they're doing." The Manager moved closer, pretending to busy herself rearranging baked goods, the barista was now trembling. "Never mind. You don't want to know. Go on with your life. Enjoy your kids. Forget I said anything."

The grinder came to a stop. The barista moved back toward the register.

"I think I know what you mean. I always thought the housewives had the harder job, you know, home with the kids all day. But lately, I don't know –"

"It's a scam. If you're pretty enough, find the right guy to twist around your finger, you never have to work again," she sneered. "Just like the Nobles and the Serfs...or was it the Lords and the Peasants? I get that confused, I never paid attention in school." Shifting gears, she played to the room. "That will be nine-fifty. Could I interest you in a Starbucks gift card?"

"Sure. Put twenty on it." I leaned in, "When does this place quiet down?"

"Your coffee and twenty on the gift card," her voice dropped to a whisper, "Come back after two. I'm here until three."

"Thanks."

She peered out of the corner of her eye at her Manager, "Thank you and come again. Have a nice day, sir."

I walked to the door, every eye in the room following me. I glanced back at the spandex clad women and smiled a broad, knowing smile, the smile of a man whose eyes were beginning to open. On the way to my car, I dug my key into the passenger door of a BMW wagon and dragged it the length of the vehicle. I made the line nice and squiggly just to be a bastard. "Kiss my ass yenta leeches." Whoever said "knowledge is power" was pretty dialed in, I'm feeling powerful this morning.

I had a pretty good idea of what kind of car to get Alicia, but I wanted to hit this mother right on the bullseye. I wanted to blow her mind. By getting the exact car she was lusting after I could shake her to the core, send her the message that I'm in the game and that I wasn't going to be a pushover anymore. So I decided to go back into the hive, to descend once again into the witches' lair – I went back to the MAC pool with determination in my heart and bad intent in my head.

Alicia and these women had no doubt discussed her wants and needs. She was probably on the phone with half of them last night. I think that these women are sharing everything with each other, sharing tips and techniques on how to manipulate their husbands. I think it's an Us versus

Them thing. Call it a neighborhood conspiracy if you want. This whole car gambit is going to prove my point.

Let's examine the facts: these women are all part of middle class or more affluent households, they don't have to work. Naturally they're going to have lots of free time to shop, play tennis and sit by the pool in addition to cooking and cleaning. Of course, most of these women have house-keepers and dine out practically every night, but let's forget that for a moment. Here's what got me so twisted up: these women are living the dream and they are ungrateful, spiteful and condescending where their husbands are concerned. Okay? Why am I so fired up? They were talking about their own husbands, not me, so why do I care? I don't know. Some unspoken bond between men maybe. These wenches were taking the piss out of their loving providers in a public setting. Maybe my sense of decency and the need for social justice was driving me or maybe it was the fear that my wife is one of them and she talks like that about me when I'm not around. I guess the thing that scared me was that the housewives seemed so coordinated. The efforts to extract wealth from their husbands were planned out, orchestrat-ed even. When my wife started dropping two ton hints about Debra and her new Mercedes, something just clicked. What if all these women were really doing was sitting around the pool all day strategizing ways to put the pinch on us and bleed us dry?

Flip-flop, flip-flop, flip-flop.

My sandals announced my arrival as I strode confidently into the inner sanctum, my Vogue magazine firmly in hand. Their lounge chairs were aimed east to catch the late morning sun. I found an empty chair in the middle of the hive and plopped my hairy ass down.

"Mornin' ladies."

Several of the women exchanged confused looks. Their faces seemed to say, "Uh, excuse me, man, what gives?" And "Who the hell does Mr. Man think he is?" and one look specifically said, "Quit staring at my perfectly enhanced rack you fat little fuck."

Kristen was the first to speak. "Uh, Hello Mike. Where's Alicia?" She stared over her designer shades.

"Don't ask me. I'm not the boss of her," I winked.

" Yes, well, are things alright? She told me you had a fight," Kristen tried to sound compassionate.

My wife told you we had a fight? Ah-hah. She was on her cell phone last night ratting me out to any house frau who would listen. I was afraid that was the case. My wife had stepped over the line – you don't air our dirty laundry with your friends. I never run Alicia down with my buddies. Where's the quid pro quo? Okay, fine then, I'm left with no choice. I had confirmed the obvious, these housewives do share everything. They are, quite likely, more closely knit with each other than they are with the men that they exchanged vows with. I decided to give them a run for their money, a brush back pitch if you will, a little high heat.

"Oh, the fight was nothing. But after the fight Alicia caught me jacking off to this porn star on Howard Stern. She was a little miffed, but what are you gonna do? Do you watch Howard, he's fucking hilarious."

Kristen's mouth fell wide open. I could feel the house-wives growing more and more uncomfortable. I had penetrated their fortress and now they didn't know what to do with me (heh, heh, he said 'penetrated'). I suppose they could hypnotize me with their "chick chatter" thing, but at the moment, they were speechless.

I turned my attentions to Debra, you know Neon Green Bikini, "Alicia did tell me about your new wheels though. Sounds like a sweet ride."

Debra studied me, trying to figure out the play.

"A Land Rover, was it?"

"A Mercedes, actually," she smiled through clenched teeth.

"Did ya catch Keith banging the maid?" I slapped her on the knee.

"I don't have a maid, Juanita is my housekeeper," she curtly corrected.

"Call her what you want, a hot tamale is still a hot tamale. Aww, come on. I'm just joshing ya a little, I know Keith is too big a pussy to fool around on you."

I was determined to push this boorish male thing to the limit, play out the crudest male stereotypes in hopes of shaking them out of their comfort zone. "Man, it's quiet. What did you do with all the kids?"

Kristen responded without looking up, "They're in the pool."

"Lifeguards do make great babysitters don't they? You guys have this thing down to a science," I nodded, impressed.

"Yes, well, we all play our part. Now if you don't

mind," sniffed the hot soccer mom known to me as Purple Tank Suit.

"My wife knows you right? What is your name again?"

"Melinda."

"That's right. Melinda...Melinda...I got nothing, Melinda what?"

"Deakins."

"Right. Darryl Deakins wife? Sure, damn girl, you look ten years younger than when I first met you and that was ten years ago. I'll bet there's a picture of you in your plastic surgeon's office with gray hair. Get it? Like Dorian Gray? It's a book." I was rolling now baby. "I'm only kidding Melinda. You look fabulous. If I didn't have this ring on my finger I'd be all over your shit, I'm totally serious."

Melinda gasped. Her face went ashen and I thought she might actually up chuck on the sun deck. At this point several weak willed housewives caved, grabbing their towels and moving briskly toward the snack bar. I took the precaution of watching them all the way to be sure they weren't circling back on my flank in some sophisticated housewife military maneuver.

"Ooops. I'll be quiet. I've got a magazine. Zip the lip," I exhaled loudly and settled back into my lounge chair. Tentatively, the women settled back down on their loungers. But I could tell from their tense body language that they were practically holding their breath until I left. Kristen just eyeballed me. I turned the pages of my Vogue, as loudly as possible, and guess what I found?

"Hey, listen to this Kristen, 'Control Your Man with Oral Sex'," I set the magazine on my lap. "How true is that? This writer went deep inside the male psyche for this one. Seriously, you go down on us and we are like robots, happy fucking robots. Yes, sir."

Kristen and Debra exchanged a look. Frankly, I expected more, but I guess I had them back on their heels.

"Hey, that reminds me of a joke. These two guys are sharing a taxi. One guy says: 'Have I told you about the worst blow job I ever had?' The second guy says: 'No, you haven't.' And the first guy says: 'It was fantastic.' A little truth in that joke there. Probably could bring about world peace. Think about it, uptight men are the ones drawing lines in the sand, setting deadlines, just think if these guys weren't so tense. I read a book once that said JFK jerked off ten times a day to relieve stress during the Cuban Missile Crisis. If you look at history, we probably avoided World War III because some babe named Natasha gave Kruschev a hummer just in the nick of time. Natasha was still on her knees when Nikita's head cleared, 'Missiles in Cuba? What the fuck am I thinking? Thank you, Natasha, you have just saved mankind'."

"Mike. What do you want?" shouted Kristen.

Her face was red, vibrating like the exploding heads in "Scanners." I have to say I was surprised I could push her to the point of pure irritation so quickly, but then again, that's always been one of my gifts. Okay, so here it was, my opening, my window of opportunity, my chance to test the strength and solidarity of this little neighborhood wives syndicate. I did my best to keep a straight face, exhaled deeply and fixed my gaze on a drain on the sun deck.

"Alright. I'm sorry. It's just that, I'm a little

embarrassed. Alicia and I…we did have a fight. I behaved badly last night and I want to make it up to her. I don't know what to do. I can't seem to say anything without sounding like a pig."

Okay Mike, raise the eyes slowly and dramatically, make eye contact…and continue.

"I know Alicia talks to you guys, would you help me?" I pleaded, pleadingly.

"What do you mean, make it up to her?" Debra took off her shades and searched my eyes like she was performing some kind of Jedi housewife mind scan. I resisted her probe and even managed to make my eyes tear up. I'm so good at this shit I'm scaring myself.

"I don't know. How can an object adequately represent the depth of one's affection? I mean, a diamond is only a rock, right? A beach house gets sand tracked all over it and you can never really get it clean. Nothing is good enough for my Alicia," I swallowed hard. Long pause… and bingo, the body language of every conspiring housewife changed instantly. Push long enough and you hit a nerve.

"I understand what you're saying, but maybe there is something special she might want?" said Debra, clearly hinting at something.

"Not that I know of and I've racked my brain. She has everything a woman could ask for, a big house with a housekeeper, four fantastic kids…and a nanny. We take three trips a year and she has shopping weekends in San Francisco with you guys. She has more jewelry than King Tut and she drives a Lexus, for God's sake." I threw up my hands. "What can I do?"

"What year is the Lexus?" wondered Melinda.

"Huh?" I played dumb.

"How long has she had the Lexus?" she asked again.

"I don't know. A couple of years, maybe three, why?"

"Does it have heated seats?" asked Debra.

"Uh, well, no. Actually, Alicia wanted the burgundy in leather with the moon roof and that model didn't have heated seats."

"Aaaahh," said Kristen.

"Aaaahhh? What's aaaahhh? She wants heated seats in her Lexus? That will make her happy and content? Heated seats?"

"There is a new Mercedes SUV that has leather and heated seats, which come standard. And it comes in a delicious color called Moondust," Melinda drooled.

"You guys sure know your cars," I said, parceling out more rope.

"I saw an advertisement in a magazine," said Melinda, whipping out a Motor Trend magazine from beneath an issue of Marie Claire.

"The Mercedes 500 SUV is probably the safest car Alicia could have to transport your children to and from school," nodded Debra.

"Seriously you guys, do you think Alicia would rather be driving the new Mercedes 500 SUV instead of her Lexus?"

"Do you really want to make things up to her?" Kristen scanned my soul with those pretty blue eyes, her skin is remarkably smooth and her hair...wait, must be strong, must resist mind probe.

"I really do," I managed.

" I know a simple, practical gift like the Mercedes 500 SUV in Moondust with leather, sunroof and heated seats would be a nice gesture," smiled Kristen.

"Okay then, it's settled."

I stood up. "I feel so close to you all now," I forced an awkward hug on Kristen and Melinda. "Thank you for reaching out to me."

As we broke our embrace, I "accidentally' dragged my hand across Melinda's left boob. She pretended not to notice and I pretended not to be shocked as hell that her boob felt real. I extended my arms and moved in on Debra, who recoiled and managed to get away with a dead fish handshake. Bitch.

I drove to the Mercedes dealership with victory in my heart. These evil conspirators had been provoked into showing their true colors. I'm really starting to see clearly now. I'm realizing that every subtle hint or casual comment that I've picked up on in the past decade had been conjured by my wife and her friends to manipulate me.

Remember that trip Larry and Kristen took to the Adriatic Sea? I knew about it two months before he did. Kristen had mentioned it to Alicia, who mentioned it to me and…and, God forgive me, I mentioned it to Larry.

"Have you been to Maui?" Larry stared at the brochure.

"Yeah. In the seventies, as a kid. When Hawaii was paradise, it was the most exotic place anyone had ever thought of and then the "Brady Bunch" did that hour long special episode with the Tiki god and all that. Opened the flood gates, tourism exploded. All because of Marcia Brady in a grass skirt," I laughed.

"Kristen and I have been wanting to get away. I've never been to Hawaii."

"Pretty crowded now I've heard. Built up. Although, people talk about the small island, no, maybe it's the big island. I don't know. One of them is supposed to be pretty good still. The rest is crowded, I guess."

"We're both getting really tired of the rain."

"Have you been to the Adriatic Sea?"

Larry squinted at his atlas, "Where the hell is that?"

"Near Greece or Malta, I think."

"I don't know. Kristen wants to go somewhere hot."

"I think it's hot there," I prompted.

"Doesn't sound hot. I don't think Kristen would like it. She wants to go somewhere stinking ass hot," Larry persisted.

"Okay, here's the thing. I wasn't supposed to say anything, but I guess Kristen told Alicia that she's always wanted to take a cruise to the Adriatic Sea."

"She has? The Adriatic Sea? She's never mentioned it." Larry seemed concerned, like there was something going on that he didn't know about. A feeling I can now fully relate too.

"I guess it's kind of expensive, though, eight grand or something."

"Yeah, that's the thing about Hawaii, not too bad a hit on the wallet. And we're really trying to get ahead on the college fund." His mouth was saying all the right things, but his head wasn't convinced. "What else did she say about it?"

"Forget I said anything, you have a plan, it's fine, how can you go wrong with Hawaii?" I backpedaled.

"But if Kristen wants to be in the Adriatic Sea then she won't enjoy Hawaii and that makes Hawaii a total waste of four grand. And if I'm going to waste four grand, why not waste it taking my wife where she wants to go?" Didn't make any sense to me, but Larry talked himself into a cruise through the Adriatic Sea.

At the time, I thought he made the right decision. Why not make Kristen happy? Now I see that I was an unwitting accomplice to the crime. These women, our loving wives, had conspired against us to get one of their own the trip that she wanted. And now they were doing it again and they were doing it to me this time. But I'm onto them and will have the proof I need to blow the lid off their "stay at home wives conspiracy." I could be on crack here but I thought that a man and wife were supposed to be partners. These sorts of issues should be worked out based on what is best for the family and for each other. If the man holds his wife in higher regard than all others and the wife holds the husband in higher regard than all others then matrimonial bliss is possible. But if the wife places her friendships with a bunch of gossipy suburban moms above her hard working man, then fucking hell, stand back cause now we're riding the greased rails straight to Hades.

August 5, 2003

Writing this in the bathroom. I made sure Alicia saw that I came in here with the sports page so she won't be suspicious about my marathon session. Wanting to throw her off my trail I told her I gave up on the memoir idea, with all the incriminating stuff in this journal I don't want her to see it now and blow my cover.

I honked the Mercedes' horn and Alicia exploded from the house like Gail Devers launching out of the starting blocks.

"Mike, what have you done?" She tried her best to act surprised, and, all things considered, it was a pretty good act. "This is unbelievable. A new Mercedes, for me? You are the best." Big wet mouth kiss. Tasty.

"Gross. Mom and Dad are screwing," said Andy, the little genius. He's twelve and apparently it's time for "the talk." Clearly he's been spending too much time with the Carpenter boy at recess again. Even the private school isn't a bio dome. Nice kid, this Carpenter, but he has two sisters in high school and the sex education trickle down theory is in full effect. Last time Andy went over to their place, he came home asking Alicia interesting questions like, "What's guy-on-guy porn?" Another time he and the Carpenter boy got into his sister's box of tampons, which they thought made great darts, very aerodynamic. Apparently, the sisters came home, caught the boys playing with the feminine hygiene projectiles and were less than pleased. That's all Andy's been able to relate to me without breaking down, clearly the Carpenter sisters meted out some kind of soul twisting psychological retribution that my boy's future therapist will probably hear about before I do.

Alicia slipped behind the wheel of the car with such ease I suspected she'd test driven this very car. "This has heated seats," Alicia beamed, feigning surprise. She turned on the heated seats and worked her bum into the leather, "How did you know that I wanted a Mercedes 500 SUV?"

"I took your picture around to every dealership in town and the Mercedes guys recognized you," I deadpanned.

Her face froze.

"Actually, I bounced the whole new car idea off a couple of your friends." I searched her face for any reaction.

"You did?" she said innocently.

Left eyebrow twitch. Rapid blink. Slight nostril flair. Pupil dilation. Yep, she was lying. Liar. Keep digging your hole sister.

"Yeah, I dropped by the Starbucks on Barnes Road –"

"The Starbucks? I thought you went…" The question betrayed her.

"But nobody was there. So I ran by the club. Your girls hit the pool pretty dog gone early."

"You can't waste the sun in Oregon," she smiled.

"They were great though, really helpful. Melinda even had an issue of Motor Trend handy. For some reason I always thought your friends were a little uptight, but we had a great hang together."

"I'm glad honey. I told you they liked you," she kissed me again.

Case closed. It's amazing how transparent the act is when you know what to look for. She didn't mention my disgusting, unruly behavior at the pool. No mention of the incessant and inappropriate oral copulation humor. There was no mention of me "accidentally" feeling up Melinda's awesome breast. I guess she took one for the team on that one. Apparently these conspiring housewives shrewdly stick to the bottom line: "honey, we got your man to buy you a new car."

I had them right where I wanted them. They think I'm a simple, piggish man, hypnotized by his own hard on and blind from watching too much sports on TV. They think they manipulated me into spending $65,000 on my wife. A favor she will, no doubt, repay at some point.

"We grant you this favor today, but one day a housewife will knock on your door, and you, in turn, will grant that housewife a favor." I wonder which one of these picture perfect housewives is the Godfather? I'll find out soon enough. They think they played me? Hah, that's what I want them to think. What they don't realize is that my play was to let them play me. So, technically, I played them. Follow? Sure I'm out sixty-five grand, but that's a small price to pay for the truth. I set the trap, placed the bait and my lovely wife and her little syndicate of blood sucking conspirators fell for it. They unwittingly exposed themselves. Their little matrix of manipulation is no longer invisible. Now we men have a chance to defend ourselves.

"Thank you for my Mercedes," she said. She really seemed to mean it too. I looked into her eyes and I swear I could read her thoughts: "That was too easy. Last time I had to blow him in the shower to get a new car. All I did this time was walk in on him while he was yanking the wiener."

"I was 'slapping the salami,' I blurted out.

"What?"

"What? Oh, nothing, you are welcome, baby. You deserve a new car."

August 6, 2003

Woke up this morning soaking wet. Either I pissed myself or somebody is fucking with me. I haven't woke up in piss since that unfortunate weekend in Vegas that is covered by the immunity of the Circle of Trust and will not be discussed in these pages. But let me say that I wish I could erase last night from my mind as well. Here's what went down.

"What should we do with the Lexus?" asked Alicia.

"Please, like you didn't know the lease was up in two months? Well, let's see here, the car is completely trashed, you're well over the mileage allowance and there's a new dent on the front fender that you forgot to mention. I guess we'll put a couple hundred into cleaning and detailing – as if steam cleaning can touch melted Kudo bars, three month old sticky soda and curdling milk – then we'll pay the mileage penalty and dump the worn out heap back at the dealership." That's what I felt like saying, what actually came out was more like: "I'll work it out with the dealership, don't you worry about it honey."

After I handed Alicia the keys to her new car I felt a sense of power that I hadn't experienced in I don't know how long. Who could argue or find fault with such an extravagant gift? I was going to be golden around the house for a while, long enough to figure out exactly how deep this conspiracy with the other housewives runs.

"Hey, I have an idea. Let's go for a drive and have some dinner?"

I looked over my brood. It's seven-thirty at night, their sweet little faces were tired, eyes not much more than slits. Timmy and Brent were staring me down like the evil kids in "Children of the Corn." Somehow, as if by black magic, I felt my sense of power drain right out of me. That sure didn't take long.

"Sure why not?" I heard myself say.

Good idea, let's take these over tired little time bombs out to a restaurant and watch them explode like the July 4th Waterfront Park fireworks spectacular. Super. Awesome. Great. The perfect end to a perfect day: I had survived the snake pit of malevolent housewives at the pool, confirmed that my wife was in league with them and then spent three relaxing hours haggling with the general manager at the Mercedes joint. Let's tempt fate by dragging the offspring into an eatery.

"Everybody into the car," cried Alicia.

The kids rushed the car like she'd called a safety blitz. Dirty feet and hands smeared all over the gorgeous leather. Juice boxes exploded like hand grenades, spraying their sticky sweetness all over the new car. Andy and Timmy gave the back seat the "trampoline test," bouncing furiously on their butts and catching enough air to bang their heads on the ceiling. Andy did it. Twice. The second time he hit with such force I expected his next words to be "I can't feel my legs, for the love of God, I can't feel my legs." Fortunately, his response was to smash Timmy on the arm with his balled fist, like it was his fault.

"Quit bouncing when I'm bouncing you little jerk," Andy spat. If the smack on the arm didn't hurt him, the spiteful words from his brother sure did and Timmy burst into tears.

"Andy, we don't talk like that to each other, especially not your brother. He's only two years younger, you'll both be in high school together and you're going to need someone to watch your back. Be nice to him. You can't treat him like that and assume he's going to be there for you forever."

Andy looks at Timmy. Timmy's eyes meet Andy, a shared moment. Yeah, sometimes I uncork some pretty good Dad speeches.

"He said ass," snickered Andy.

"I ass-umed he said ass," Timmy giggled. They both exploded into laughter. Don't you love brothers, there's nothing like them. Beating the crap out of each other one second, united against the world the next.

Meanwhile, Cassie and Brent have ingeniously turned their Juicy Juice boxes into squirt guns. Anyone can play, simply aim your straw at the target and squeeze violently and a purple stream of juice sprays out with the force of a fire hose. Cassie sprays Brent. Giggle. Brent sprays Cassie. Giggle. Cassie sprays Brent. Giggle. Brent sprays Cassie. Giggle. Cassie tries to spray Brent. Nothing. Sobs.

"Daddy, my Juicy Juice is broke."

"No baby, the juice is all gone." Eight fluid ounces now seeping through the complimentary floor mats and into the upholstery of this brand spanking new Mercedes 500 SUV. In five minutes my little lovelies have taken twenty grand off the value of this fine automobile. They are as efficient as a school of piranhas stripping a goat's carcass clean.

"Can I have more Juicy Juice?" Cassie asked innocently.

"Let's wait until we get to the restaurant," Alicia said. "Baby, give me a minute, I have to powder my nose." Alicia disappeared, leaving me trapped in the car with the four human explosive devices.

Yeah, wait until we get to the restaurant...now I see where she's going with this, she's probing for my breaking point. Yeah, let's go have an elegant dinner out with four kids and drain every ounce of patience from me. She's trying to break my spirit. I give her a car and she immediately throws a brush back pitch as if to say, "Thanks for the car, but it don't change a thing, baby."

Maybe I didn't understand her strategy before but I can see it plain as day now. I think back over our long history of "dynamite dinners." You know, when your children are powder kegs just waiting for a spark, and you take them out to dinner anyway? See if this sounds familiar: you put in a ten, twelve, fourteen hour day on the factory floor or in an office full of assholes. You bust your hump all day negotiating a new contract or pitching a big client or trying to produce your quota, then you grind through the monotonous commute, narrowly avoiding decapitation at the hands of a blind trucker. When at last you reach home, your only desire is to suck on a cold Bud and flip on Sportscenter. After a day in the salt mines, providing for your family, it's not outrageous to ask for a little "me" time and cocktail peanuts, is it? But here's how it goes:

"Hey babe, you're late," your wife points out.

"Today was a killer. I had to review the quarterly

projections with Straussman, for the third time. Then there was a freaking oil tanker overturned on the interstate."

She nods blankly, not hearing a single word you've said, "Uh-huh, I thought maybe we could go out for a quick bite," she smiles sweetly.

Oh sure, 'a quick bite', a little romantic snack…with four kids in tow?

"I don't know baby," I lowered my eyes, crossed my arms and leaned back against the fridge with a sigh, the most obvious 'I don't want to go out for dinner' body language I could come up with.

"I've been cooped up in this house with the kids all day by myself, you know," she said finally. Well there it is, she's breaking out the big guns. I'm tempted to point out that for six hours the kids were at school, so "all day" is a bit of an exaggeration, while I, on the other hand, did actually work "all day."

"Besides, we don't have anything in the house, I'll have to run to the store if you expect me to make dinner," she sniffed.

Now the first thought I have is, "You didn't go to the motherfucking store? What in the hell did you do all day?" Even with a round of golf, a manicure and two, no, three hours for coffee with the girls there still must be time to swing by the grocery and pick up something for dinner.

Wisely, I hold my tongue and do the math: ten exhausting minutes trying to agree on what to have for dinner, twenty five minutes for her to run to the store and back, thirty five minutes if she sees someone she knows, and another half hour for meal preparation. All told we're looking at an hour before food hits my face. She's got me and she knows it. It's actually faster to go out to dinner, and then you get a look at the kid's expectant faces. You know she's primed them with "When Daddy finally gets his lazy ass home he's taking us all out to dinner." They look up at you like grungy orphans.

"Okay, sure, why not? Let's go out to dinner," I sigh.

I'm always amazed when my mouth betrays my body with those words. I want to say "no, let's order a pizza." And I could probably sell that to the kids, but that would be an overt act of war akin to moving troops into the Sudatenland or killing that pig on the Canada-Washington state border. I wouldn't get a slice of 'za while it was still hot, because I'd be too busy fighting. And there's always the chance that she's programmed the kids like in the "Manchurian Candidate" – they'd hear the phrase "How about a pizza?" and they'd go freak city. No, I'm not falling into the pizza trap. Nice try.

I do think there is some kind of psychic grind that the wife lays on me, a form of mind control that manipulates my analytical male mind. I examine all the options, as she knows I will, and, somehow I still conclude that going out to dinner is the best of the possible scenarios. I suppose if I concluded anything else, it'd be because that's what she wants me to conclude. Damn, she's good.

Alicia finally emerges from the house. Funny, her nose doesn't look powdered, what has she been doing in there? Maybe she was squeezing out a man-sized growler – that image makes me laugh. If "powder my nose" really means "I gotta take a hanging shit," I wish women would come out and say it. They're always begging for more "openness" and "honesty" in our relationships. Guess what boys? It's all a smoke screen.

"How does 'The Ringside' sound?" My delivery is casual and offhand, as if trying to sneak an off speed pitch past a fastball hitter. The Ringside is a classic in Portland. Fantastic steaks, the rib eye cut being my personal favorite, killer onion rings and, best of all, a bar where all the old money goes to puff on cigars. If I time it just right, I can sneak into the lounge, break out a Cuban and catch an inning of the Mariner game about the time Cassie will be pouring ice water on her head.

"No, that place is too dark. Let's go over to Chili's." Shot down in flames. She fires up the Mercedes. I notice her lips curl up in a smile of pure satisfaction.

"Good evening, welcome to Chili's. Six for dinner?" The words were barely out of her mouth, before the color drained from the face of the hostess. Andy, Cassie, Timmy and Brent might as well have been the Four Horsemen of the Apocalypse. At first the hostess was confused, then her gaze became a mix of pity and terror. She knew what was to come, it had been prophesized in the stars. And, she'd been working at Chili's since last summer and knew a meltdown waiting to happen when she saw one. Four red eyed kids walk in at seven forty five at night, the video arcade is out of order and the Dad doesn't want to be there. The hostess led us to our table like she was leading us to our doom. She then tossed crayons on the table and quickly retracted her hand like she was tossing raw meat into the tiger cage.

The meal was a slow motion disaster. I've been in car crashes that took less time, you know, the kind where you watch the jackhole run the red light, aim his bumper right at you and it feels like a half hour before the metal starts to twist.

Alicia ordered the Fajitas. Fine right? Wrong. The steaming vegetables come to your table in a hot iron skillet. The waitress announces the arrival with the customary 'Hot plate' greeting. Andy waited almost three seconds before touching the skillet and started howling like a wounded animal. He rolled around the booth in such agony that I considered tearing off his entire arm to lessen the pain.

One down.

But I wasn't going down that easy. I patted Andy encouragingly and then ignored him. I smiled at Alicia, "How are your fajitas honey?"

"Great. I love this place. Not too fancy, but the food's good. How is your steak?"

"Good, it's good," I lied. With each bite I tried to convince myself that I was actually eating my rib eye steak from Ringside, but Andy's periodic wailing kept breaking my concentration. How can Alicia block out the sobbing and sniffling? I pretended not to notice that the poor kid has snot running from his nose and every thirty seconds or so he sucks it all back into his sinus cavity with a mighty, sloppy snort.

Timmy's chicken fingers arrived and, despite ordering chicken fingers at every single meal we've ever eaten out, he somehow seemed surprised.

"I don't want these," he said.

"Hey buddy, they're chicken fingers. It's alright, they look yummy," I cajoled.

Timmy waved one under his nose, sniffing intently. "No they don't. They cooked them wrong."

"What do you mean?" I opened the can of worms.

"They're all dirty."

"Dirty?"

"See? They have dirt all over them," he pointed out bits of seasoning that covered the chicken fingers. "I can't eat the dirt. And don't try to tell me it's pepper. It's not pepper, it's dirt."

I spent the next ten minutes of my life picking microscopic bits of seasoning off the fucking chicken fingers. "There you go buddy," I mussed his hair in that way that makes me feel fatherly.

"I hate this place," he said to no one in particular. Timmy pouted and sucked on one chicken finger like a lollypop for the rest of the evening.

Two down.

"Do you want some of my chicken? I'll never eat all this," Alicia proclaimed.

"You could take it home and have it for lunch."

"That's okay, I'm having lunch with Kristen tomorrow. I promised her a ride in my new Mercedes."

"When did you talk to Kristen?"

"Last night when we were fighting –"

"Last night?"

"I mean tonight, when I ran inside to powder my nose," she looked away quickly.

"Oh, yeah, tonight," I nodded. Hell, if she's gonna be that sloppy and practically confess, where's the fun in this? She and Kristen talked about tricking me into buying the car last night? Old news girlfriend, but let's see you wrangle anything more than a trim at Super Cuts from here on out.

Brent, God love him, had the decency to fall asleep in his food – face first. The bun of his hamburger made a great pillow. He only stirred when the still blubbering Andy stole some fries from him. "Dad, he's eating my dinner. Make him eat his own dinner. He's taking my dinner," the semi-conscious Brent moaned, before going back to sleep on his cracked wheat bun.

Three down.

Alicia continued to pretend that she was enjoying the meal of a lifetime. Shit, if you're going to work that hard at it, what's the point? "I'm going to order another margarita, do you mind driving home?" she said.

"I don't mind, drink up," I urged. Her Zen like ability to focus on her meal and block out the kids was amazing. Maybe she's already drunk. Even if I was bombed I couldn't ignore this four ring circus performing in our booth. Apparently, the other patrons can't block it out either, they're fleeing from our section like refugees. Clearly, Alicia and I were having a battle of wills. She was determined to enjoy her meal and, in doing so, snap my will in half. Understanding the challenge, I was determined not to crack first. I wouldn't be the first to lose my temper. I wouldn't be the first to raise my voice. I battled to hang on, I swear to you I did.

Cassie, my little angel, light of my life, dainty princess, had been sneaking sips of my Coke and was now eight miles high. She bounced around the booth like a Chinese fucking acrobat. She'd eat a bite and do a somersault. She'd eat another bite and do a round off. She'd swallow some more food and do a back hand spring. What, is she trying to qualify for the Olympics here or what? She gulped down her lemonade, inhaled her french fries, chomped on Andy's burger, scarfed her own cheese sandwich and then – launched all of it in an impressive display of projectile vomiting. The East German judge gives her a perfect ten.

Four down.

The creamy splatter elicited a shriek from some fat blue hair at the next table, who quickly fled. The shriek in turn woke Brent. "Cassie barfed on my dinner. Why can't she barf on her own dinner? She barfed all over my dinner."

Cassie launched another impressive load, this time narrowly missing Andy. Andy started to cry hard again.

"What are you crying for? You're not the one spewing your dinner, honey."

"I burned my hand."

"That was forty five minutes ago," I calmly pointed out.

"It hurts. Don't you care? Don't you love me?"

Not now kid. This is not the time to start milking it.

Cassie crawled toward me, "Daddy, I'm sick." Woof. Half eaten burger and Coke splashed onto my lap. A moment later the smell hit me. Wet egg salad. Why does puke always smell like egg salad? No matter what you ate, it always comes up smelling like egg salad. I stared at my lap. I noticed that my little princess didn't chew her food all that well, I'll have to speak to her about that later. Out of the corner of my eye I swear I saw a little smile begin to creep onto Alicia's face. Not a full smile, no teeth, but just the hint of the slightest upturn at the corners of her mouth. She knew victory would be hers and she couldn't wait to celebrate. It was that damn smile of satisfaction again.

Right about there I snapped.

"Okay, that's it. We're out of here. Let's go," I shouted.

"Just take her to the bathroom Mike," Alicia said quietly, baiting me. Was she crazy? Was she piling on? I think she was piling on.

"Get a doggie bag. We're going," I bellowed.

Five down. She got me.

And, as much as I'm embarrassed to say it – it felt good. I felt like Pacino in "Dog Day Afternoon." I was calling the shots and everyone was going to damn well do whatever the fuck I said. Never mind that this was exactly the reaction I was trying to avoid. Never mind that this was exactly the reaction Alicia was hoping for. I know it's a sin, but being the "Mad Dad" felt good. I had lost the contest, but blowing off a little steam seemed a fine consolation prize.

"I'm not finished, Dad," said Brent, who had little creases on his face from his bun/pillow.

"NOW!" I grabbed his arm and lifted him out of the booth and onto his feet.

I can't remember what else I said. I may have muttered some expletives. I know I offered a twenty dollar apology to the waitress, but she only glared at me, offended at the way I "handled" my "cute kids." The escape from the restaurant was a blur of vomit, crying kids and judgmental patrons. But I understand, I mean, really, who wants their dinner ruined by some idiot dragging his children out of the restaurant.

"Why aren't those kids home in bed?" an old guy commented.

"Quit sucking up to your ball and chain, traitor, you know damn well this wasn't my idea," I shot back.

"That poor mother, having to put up with that ogre," another woman muttered. Okay, let's have it people, give the dead horse a good kick.

In the parking lot, Alicia huffed along behind me as if this debacle had been my fault. She didn't say a word on the way home. Her silence indicting me for losing it with the children. And I did lose it. But, isn't that entrapment or something? If the undercover vice squad comes in, sets a dime bag on the table and you pick it up – they can't arrest you, can they? Crockett, Tubbs, where are you guys? Explain the rules to my wife, will ya?

I parked the Mercedes in our driveway. By the way, it handles beautifully for an SUV, I could get used to that ride. Thank goodness she didn't want a Hummer.

"Thanks for a lovely evening," Alicia scowled. "Come on kids."

So there it is, I buy my wife a new car and I'm still sleeping on the couch.

I mull over all the shit I've learned in the past couple of days. I realize there is more going on here than I understand. It seems that my marriage, my relationship is a game, a contest. But I don't know what the rules are and without any real experience playing this game, I know I'm a heavy underdog. But I'm not afraid of being the underdog. The 1968 New York Jets were underdogs, the 1969 Amazing Mets were underdogs, Doug Flutie has been an underdog his whole career and Buster Douglas was an underdog when he dropped Iron Mike Tyson. I know I'm not going to win this thing on a decision. My best shot is to take my beating and hang around until the late rounds and go for the knockout.

August 7, 2003

Cruised over to MLK Boulevard and turned in the Lexus today. Ouch! What a shot in the shorts that was. For $5,800 in mileage penalties and damages, I probably should've totaled the rig on the way over and let insurance take care of it. Actually, the interior was close to totaled. Apparently, the kids had been exploring their inner children through "food awareness art therapy" for the past forty-four months – the guy at the dealership thought the backseat looked like a Jackson Pollack painting. Hey, don't think I'm a fag or something, Alicia rented a movie about him. The dude who was in "The Right Stuff" played this fucked up, crazy painter. He was really good too, I almost slit my wrists watching it.

Drove back over to the Starbucks on Barnes Road to find that barista who had been so talkative the other day. I intended to follow up with my informant sooner, but things have been fast and furious.

I stepped into the rarified coffee air and surveyed the crowd. Housewives, in packs of three or four, crowded around the tables chatting with the fervor of insurgents plotting an assassination. For all I knew, they were. And, dammit to hell, it was loud. How could they hear themselves think? Heck, how could they even hear themselves talk? Each table was louder than the next. Their words swirled around my head – I shook them off and pushed forward, scanning the coffee shop for my informant. No sign of her. Maybe she was in the back. I reached the register and was greeted by Kim, a blonde barista in a baseball cap.

"I'll take a coffee, black. With no fancy shit in it."

The blonde barista regarded me with suspicion, after all, who the hell goes into a Starbucks and orders a plain coffee?

"I was wondering if, oh, what's her name, the brunette with the nose piercing was working today?" I kept my voice low, but friendly.

Her eyes narrowed.

"You know, spunky girl, generally works mornings?" I continued.

"I guess I don't know who you mean," she said haltingly.

"I wish I could remember her name. There's an "a" in it, though. She circled the "a," like an "anarchy" symbol. How many clerks here do that?" I pressed.

The blonde barista began to get twitchy, "Okay, she doesn't work here anymore," she sputtered.

"She doesn't work here anymore? Since when?"

The Manager approached, and slammed my cup down on the counter slopping scalding coffee onto my hand. "Here's your coffee, sir. Thanks for your patronage." Those were her words, but her tone said "You don't have to go home but you can't stay here."

"I was looking for a clerk, I guess an ex-clerk –"

"You mean to say a 'barista,' that's what we call our associates," she corrected. She gestured to the blonde barista, who scurried off to the storage room.

"Yeah, well. I need to find the punky little brunette who worked mornings."

"I don't recall an employee who fits that description," the Manager said.

"She sure as hell ground me a pound of coffee two days ago."

"Is there a problem? I'd be happy to help you."

"Yeah, I want to see the 'barista' with the nose piercing."

"Sir, I'd like to help you, but I don't have any idea what you're talking about here," she insisted.

"Your other girl said she didn't work here anymore. Let me talk to her again."

"Please, I have other customers. Drive safely," the Manager smiled and moved off.

I sat down at the only open table in the place and waited for the blonde barista to emerge from the back room. I sipped my coffee, slowly at first, testing for strychnine. What was the real story here? Where was my informant? Did she quit? Was she transferred? Were they holding out on me because I was old enough to be her father's "bad friend" from the army? Or, hang on a minute, was the punky barista fired because she talked to me? Or, worse still, had she been "disappeared" by these housewives because she was a security threat? Working in a place like this she must be privy to all kinds of dark housewife secrets and nefarious housewife plots. The barista was bitter, resentful and ready to spill it all to me so they got rid of her. Oh sure, she could've simply lost her temper and spit in the latte of some uppity housewife and been shit canned. No, that's what the housewives would want me to think. Remember what we've learned: there's always something going on that we can't see.

The noise in this Starbucks is deafening. Cheesy, broken hearted music by Natalie Merchant or Sarah

McLachlan or some other sad, depressed chick seeps out of the overhead speakers. Squealing kids run laps around the tables. One little girl chases another with the sugar container, leaving a trail of white powder behind her. A little boy has the non-fat milk thermos in one hand, the two-percent milk in the other and is bashing them together making robot noises. Crash after crash, "Zoltron" battled "Robotor" until the top pops off and non-fat "hydraulic fluid" drains out all over my shoes. Tough break "Robotor," all hail lord "Zoltron."

Who do these kids belong to anyway? I haven't seen a single housewife make eye contact with any of these kids since I walked in. And where the hell is the blonde barista? Did they stuff her in a barrel and roll her out the back so she won't talk to me either? The mind numbing chatter of twenty separate conversations bleeding into one is causing my brain to go fuzzy. I try to focus on a single conversation but the housewives have put up their Jedi housewife Veil of Babble. I hear words, but they're coming out of sequence or something.

"Store remember Chi next this until go tea the by at," one housewife exclaimed.

"Blue for dress way me excitement store five," replied another.

Is this a new dialect of their secret language? I haven't figured out if these house fraus have actually developed their own version of "pig Latin" or if they're able to put me under with some mild form of hypnosis. The mildest form being where the wife starts talking and you get instantly bored and are unable to listen or care what she's saying.

That would explain why men can't follow anything the women say. And, I have to admit, it's funny: they're babbling, with the sole intent of hypnotizing us, and then they yell at us for not paying attention to them. "I can't pay attention when you're hypnotizing me woman!" No wonder they get bored with us – we're no challenge.

My heart lifts momentarily as two guys walk into the Starbucks. Brothers in arms, we'll unite and ransack this female strong hold. But they order a pair of Caramel Mochas and race out the door faster than Jeff Gordon gets in and out of the pit. The skinny dude had to ask three times for an insulated sleeve – he kept passing the hot coffee from hand to hand until the Manager finally relented. Cowards.

Here's another thing, most of these housewives are drinking Chai Tea. I'm not sure I've ever seen a guy drinking Chai Tea. I know the baristas have never offered me a Chai Tea. "Try the Frappacino, try the caramel mocha, try the Breakfast Blend," but never "Try the Chai Tea." Why is that? Is it against some code of conduct, some secret alliance between Starbucks and these housewives? Maybe men will break out in hives if we drink their precious Chai Tea, maybe there is a special herbal blend designed to evoke an allergic reaction in men? Or maybe the Chai Tea is some sort of brain booster that heightens a woman's ability to control our minds. The person who started the largest Chai Tea company in America is a woman, she sold her product to Starbucks, which happens to be the single most popular gathering spot for women in America. Coincidence? I don't think so. Alright, I admit I'm not making much sense here. I've got to get out of this place before my head explodes from all this chick chatter.

Did these housewives conspire to "disappear" the punky barista? Could they do that, really? Can they exert pressure, corporately, on individuals who are not in their direct circle of influence? That girl didn't live in this neighborhood. Can they reach outside of our neighborhood? I know the housewives communicate amongst themselves, I have proof of that. I'm sure they can influence and get members of their little evil housewife clique to do the bidding of the group. But if these housewives can reach beyond their membership, if they can reach out and exert their will on the general public then we're talking about a highly evolved and organized entity with limitless power. We're talking about a full-blown housewife mafia operating in my neighborhood. Of course, we all know that the mafia doesn't exist and that John Gotti is simply one hell of a plumber.

If I can't get any info from the now missing barista, I'll have to find it somewhere else. I need to know what we're really up against here, find out how deep this thing goes.

August 8, 2003

Trying to play it cool around the house. Alicia has been a bit distant the past couple of days. I guess she's not used to me being around the house so much or maybe I tipped my hand too quickly. She let me sleep in our marital bed last night, but things still feel a bit icy. She's invited Jim and Susie Holcomb for dinner tonight. I'm going to try and get Jim alone and see what he knows. Maybe my free time gives me an advantage over the other men – I've seen things they haven't – but if this neighborhood is really being run by these housewives there must be other witnesses. It's them, right? It's not me, it's them, right?

Seems so weird, fifteen years down the line with my wife and to be so suspicious of her intentions. How could I think she's part of some conspiracy? Alicia was my ideal woman: Smart, funny, beautiful, a great lover, a generous partner…or at least that's how it started.

When we started dating I couldn't believe that Alicia was interested in me. She was a junior lawyer in a small firm but everyone knew she was going to write her own ticket. She was bright, hardworking and had a competitive edge to her – she liked to win. I was stumbling around in dead end marketing jobs, making decent money and picking up the business experience that would later pay off with my Internet company, BrownBox.com (damn, that was a good name).

Alicia accepted my proposal on the docks at River Place on a warm June afternoon. I spent practically everything I had on that ring. I even sold an old Triumph Spitfire that I'd bought in high school. Occasionally, I'd pick up a spare part at an auto show in hopes of resurrecting this sweet ride to its former glory. Never really got around to it, but selling it felt like getting punched out in front of your girlfriend. Actually, it felt worse than that, more like, say, getting busy in the back of the limo with your prom date and discovering the French exchange student Rene is a guy.

But selling the Spitfire had to be done. A collector gave me $4,500 for it. I think he overpaid. Maybe he felt sorry for me because he knew I was selling my baby to buy a girl a ring. It's funny, to this day I remember how sad the collector looked.

"Good luck, kid. I hope it works out," he said.

"Yeah, are you, did you, uh…" I stammered.

"Still am. Thirty-seven years, that's why I'm saying 'good luck'," he smiled bitterly.

I remember thinking, "Poor guy, he must've married the wrong girl or got the mayor's daughter pregnant or something." Now I curse that old bastard for not filling me in on the score.

Alicia and I were married the following spring. By then I had landed a solid PR job with KEX radio and always managed to scrounge up free Blazer tickets. Clyde Drexler, Jerome Kersey, Kevin Duckworth, Buck Williams and Terry Porter, now that was a basketball team. They played beautiful ball, were good community guys and Rip City loved them. Those guys nearly resurrected the Blazers' golden years when Bill Walton, Mo "The Enforcer" Lucas, Bobby Gross, Dave Twardzik, Lionel Hollins and Dr. Jack Ramsay brought the city their only major sports championship. Looking back I equate my best days with those of the Blazers in the late eighties and early nineties. When they were rolling through the Western Conference, kicking Laker ass and going to the Finals, things were perfect with Alicia and I. Of course, the Pistons and the Bulls smacked Portland in the NBA Finals in 1990 and 1992, maybe I should've taken that as a sign. We bought our first house, a big, funky, old one in the Alameda neighborhood of Northeast Portland. Alicia tastefully decorated the house with a bunch of fussy, expensive Ethan Allen furniture – most of it was stuff I was afraid to get dirty. Then she promptly announced that I'd knocked her up and now she wanted to leave the firm and start a family. I was stunned. Where was my booty-kicking career woman? Uh, how were we going to pay for this big house and all this new furniture and shit without her income? I'm going to be someone's Dad? Are you shitting me? Shouldn't we have talked about this?

"That's great honey," was all I could manage.

I guess I shouldn't have been surprised. Alicia had been a freak in the sack recently and had quit being a nag about using rubbers. She was saying stuff like "I'm hot for your man meat," but I should've translated that to "I want a baby, Mike."

Really, Alicia has never been more passionate than when she was trying to extract my seed from me. Some primal shit going on there. "I want the fast swimmers, Mike. Give me seven million of the fast ones," she would moan. Sounded sexy at the time, I guess you had to be there. But when my woman starts talking like that my caveman DNA kicks into gear and I explode like a fire extinguisher. "Here come seven million of my best, baby." In that moment, my only purpose on this planet is to fertilize her egg. My tribe must survive and the more children I sire the better my tribe's chances for survival are.

I would have been a good Caveman, I think. Life was simple for the Caveman, he had it made – spending all day dragging cave women around by their hair, banging all the good looking ones, fighting dinosaurs, discovering fire – what a life. And when the cave gets full of little cave kids, the Caveman would go out hunting and gathering. If the clan really got annoying, the Caveman could go on a "business trip," a quest for more fire or a new water source or to rescue some careless cave kid that got carried off by a Pterodactyl.

Funny, as I write that, things aren't all that different today, are they? The caves now come with mortgages, Brontosaurus meat is nineteen dollars a pound at the designer grocery, and the quest for fire each day requires a forty-five minute commute. Same shit, different age, huh?

On the bright side, Alicia and I have four kids and it took several tries to get each kid, so I do have some killer memories. But isn't it brutal to compare the over heated scrogging of a babe trying to get knocked up with that of a housewife simply lying back to do her "duty for Mother England"? It's almost cruel really, our women show us how great sex can be and then so rarely deliver the goods. Would almost be better not to know. As good as our occasional sex is now, in some quiet place in my heart I can't help but be disappointed because I know she didn't give it her all. But we keep coming back just in case, don't we?

"She only loves me for my sperm" bounces around in the back of my head from time to time. Now, with these new developments, these random thoughts and memories are starting to connect. The old car collector, what did he know? Why did my wife abruptly turn from professional to homemaker? Was that all part of her plan or was she recruited by some evil housewife who turned her to the dark side?

With the arrival of Andy, a mighty fire was lit under my ass, out of pure terror I began to work like never before. It soon became clear that I wouldn't be able to support my new family on a traditional salary and that led to the formation of my own PR company. Here's the irony, if Alicia would have continued her career in law, I probably would've been content hanging out at the radio station and hawking my Blazer comps when I needed some fast cash. Ultimately, she's more responsible for our cat bird seat today than I am, she provided the motivation. I'm retired at 38, but right now I'm feeling more like a puppet than a Business Week cover boy.

August 9, 2003

I'm scrawling this entry in the bathroom again, trying to buy a little time. Alicia has got me running the kids all around today so she can get her hair done. She's been busting my balls ever since I bought her the Mercedes. She pretends to be helpful, suggesting things to do to help me pass my time, but I think she's fucking with my head. My "Honey Do" list seems to grow each day and she's pulling stuff out of her ass to keep me busy. Here's what she's got me doing today:

MIKE'S WIFE MANDATED TO DO LIST:

Drop Cassie off for her play date at Kristen's

First off, it's summer, who the hell needs a play date? What ever happened to kicking the kids outside and letting them find a vacant lot to play in? Let them make their own fun like throwing rocks at old Coke bottles. This play date shit is stunting their growth if you ask me. And there are going to be eight kids at the play date. If you do the math you'll realize that there are now seven housewives loose in the neighborhood, plotting pedicures and who knows what other malice.

Mow Lawn

Now she's being vindictive. I tried to remind her that I hired a gardener, at her insistence, and she starts yelling at me, "You never help around the house." Okay, honey, whatever. At least I'll finally get to drive that bad boy John Deere riding mower. Never mind that my back yard is ten feet by twenty, with a steep embankment. If I get the mower going fast enough maybe I can roll the thing.

Take Andy to Dermatologist

After she saw the "20/20" segment on skin cancer, Alicia has been out of her mind. I tried to tell her that Andy has freckles, she keeps calling them "malignant moles." I'm all for getting the most out of my insurance plan, but I looked close at his face and I swear Alicia drew the mole on with a Magic Marker.

Take the Kids Swimming

I'm a little nervous about returning to the Witch's Lair. When the house fraus are massed in such a big group I think their power is greater. But at least this will give me a chance to spy on these conspiring housewives. Of course, Alicia's probably sending me there so her cohorts can keep an eye on me.

Go to Value Village for a vintage Postal Carrier jacket.

Huh? I had to ask about this one. Turns out Alicia is planning our neighborhood Halloween party and thinks a "Tribute to Civil Servants" is a great theme. "Can't this wait?" I asked her and I got a lecture on responsibility and proper planning. You'd think I'd learn not to ask questions. The theme is growing on me however, I'm either going to break out the white shirt, black tie and black slacks and go as an IRS accountant or get the Postal Carrier jacket and an Uzi and go as a disgruntled and homicidal mailman.

Pick up Five hundred pounds of Bark

Again, I play the "but we have a gardener" card – no go. We had the gardener roto-till the side yard with intention of planting a small vegetable garden, but now Alicia wants to bag that idea and just cover it with wood chips. I do talk her into letting me pick up the bark in her new Mercedes SUV – so at least I'll get to haul something around in that giant car besides kids. My own little subversive victory…of course, that means she's driving my Porsche around all day. Damn. I'm tired of getting jobbed.

Rent "Steel Magnolias"

This seems solely designed to humiliate. "Steel Magnolias?" Seriously? Olympia Dukakis and a dying Julia Roberts? What if someone sees me? "If that's checked out get 'Terms of Endearment' or 'Beaches'," she said. She may have overplayed her hand here. I can see this coming. She and her girlfriends have already checked these movies out and they're setting me up for the humiliation of asking for every fucking chick flick ever made. The greasy haired punk with the lip ring will be shaking his head at me saying, "Dude, we have "House of a Thousand Corpses." And I'll have to say, "What about 'The Divine Secrets of the Ya-Ya Sisterhood'?" and finally he'll say, "Are you some kind of queer fag?" and I'll have to say, "Yeah, I guess am."

Pick up Fresh Fish for Dinner

Okay, that seems fine, at least I know we'll have something in the house for dinner and I'll be able to choose what I want. Of course, whatever I choose Alicia won't be happy with. This is a little game I know. If I bring home salmon, she'll want cod, and vice versa.

Buy Timmy P.E. Shoes

What the hell has she been doing with her time? Not much I guess, she's been freaking coasting for the last week. Maybe she's trying to make the point that she's a busy woman and my retirement isn't going to be spent playing golf every day. Maybe she's trying to get me to walk a mile in her pumps. Nice try, Timmy shows me six pairs of Nikes in his closet. They all have non-marking soles and would be appropriate for any physical education class.

Return Makeup to Nordstrom

Now she's piling on. I suspect Alicia added this just to have ten items on the to do list, like that's some kind of rule. Here's the play: She's used up half of this container of foundation make-up and decides it makes her look too pale – and then wants me to return it for her. She knows those chicks in the Clinique lab coats freak me out. They all kind of look the same, like those hot clone babes in that old Robert Palmer video for "Addicted to Love." They have such attitude too, like once they put on those lab coats they're suddenly rocket scientists and the only ones capable of understanding the complex chemistry of cosmetics.

If Alicia's going to dump a "to do" list like this on me everyday, I'm going to have to figure out a way to take back control of my own schedule. I study the list and recognize the little traps laid for me therein. For example, the eighth chore on the list is pick up fresh fish, then chores nine and ten send me out to the Lloyd Center Mall – where that fresh fish would bake in the hot car and be spoiled when I get home. Ah-hah, gotcha. I know I'm still a move or two behind, but I'm learning how to play the game.

August 10, 2003

A moment to breathe. I think I surprised Alicia by smoothly accomplishing her enormous "Honey Do" list without a single complaint or error. I played it casually, made it sound like she missed out on some serious quality time with the kids. I even went by the salon where she had her hair done and interviewed the hairdresser. I tipped the girl fifty bucks to tell me everything she did to my wife's hair. When I got home I expertly complimented Alicia on her fabulous new hairstyle.

"Hey baby, your hair looks great," I kissed her.

"I don't know. Do you think it's too short?" She tossed out the bait.

"Too short? No. What'd she take off, about three quarters of an inch? Nah, that's just a nice clean up to eliminate the split ends. I think your hair looks more healthy, more alive."

She was thrown. Her little script of set up questions would have to be abandoned, she was going off book now – let's see how she is at improv.

"Look at me Mike. What do you think? I might go back and have her re-do it. Should I?" she teased.

"Re-do it? Why? You look beautiful. The auburn high-lights are subtle and add a rich texture. And, frankly, the slightly darker hair color compliments your skin tone." I sounded like a damn women's magazine.

"You really like it?" she asked.

"Yeah, I do. The little flecks of honey blonde are a nice touch too. They add a touch of pizzazz that really brings out your eyes," I smiled sincerely. "Your girl is good, she didn't over do it."

"It cost two hundred and sixty dollars," she smirked.

"You're worth it baby," I kissed her and went to the fridge to grab a beer.

Alicia's eyes followed me. She was half-pleased that I thought she looked good – and she did look good – and half-suspicious. "Subtle and rich texture?" Maybe I laid it on a little bit thick, but I was going for the win. I left the room whistling. I could feel her eyes on my back. Point for Mike.

Should catch you up on our dinner with Jim and Susie Holcomb the other night. They brought their two kids, both disrespecting little hoodlums if you want my personal opinion. The two women huddled in the kitchen as Jim and I hung out on the patio and barbecued some steaks and burgers. The kids ran loose in the yard, in the house, in the street, in the neighbor's yard and, for a brief moment, on the roof.

Funny how you can take four nice kids (mine) and put them together with two wild maniacs (theirs) and suddenly you have six crazy lunatics on your hands. I could have intervened I guess, but if their shenanigans weren't going to bother the ladies, then they weren't going to bother me either. Two can play that game. Besides, this gave me some time with Jim.

A little about Jim and Susie, to give you a context for their relationship: the bottom line is that she runs the whole deal and has kicked Jim's ass into submission. Long ago he gave up the fight and gave up looking for the jar that Susie hid his balls in. He's a longtime engineer with Intel, makes solid money, and when the company started to rocket in the nineties, he picked up a big ol' pile of company stock. They were riding high for a while but when the Intel stock shit itself, he was just another guy working for a paycheck. They were still in their good sized Brady Bunch house in Beaverton, but Susie wanted to be on a lake or a cliff somewhere. Despite his steady, gainful employment, Jim hasn't given Susie the star-spangled ride that she was expecting when she signed on with him. Of course, even as Susie lusts for a newer status car and bigger house, there is no way she's going to help earn the money to pay for those upgrades. She'd rather bitch at Jim about all the things he's not providing.

Jim is a sweet, quiet engineer type who loathes confrontation and is no match for the intense and articulate Susie. Instead of standing up for himself, he feels guilty and apologizes for his perceived shortcomings. She's pummeled this poor guy until he's accepted that everything wrong with her world is his fault.

As for Susie, she plays her part to the hilt: a committee hound at the Multnomah Athletic Club, she sits on the Doernbecher Children's Hospital Board and rubs elbows with Portland's rich and elite as if they were her peers. Jim's fretting about a second mortgage while Susie publicly donates ten grand to charity and then milks it for all she's worth. They're walking in separate worlds. Jim doesn't dig the scene and Susie is embarrassed that Jim is a little dweeb, not some flamboyant and influential CEO. I don't have any proof, but I'll lay odds that she's gotten her rocks off with a couple of the three piece suit types she mingles with at these big wheel functions. I've been roped into a couple of these charity deals myself and am happy to write the check "for the kids," but watching these rich pricks pat themselves on the back all night gives me the dry heaves.

I'm hoping that Jim will be able to grasp the mind-blowing reality I'm about to share with him. I almost feel like I'm in an old Twilight Zone episode:

"Jim?"

"Yeah?"

"We've known each other a long time, right?"

"Thirteen years."

"I don't know how to say this, but, we're actually robots!"

"No, shit, we're robots?"

"And this planet that we live on…"

"Yeah?"

"It's not really earth," I said.

"No way. I didn't see that twist ending coming."

That's what if feels like to me anyway. I flip over the burgers and casually lay the groundwork for my big revelation.

"How's it hanging, Jim?"

"Pretty well, I guess," he replies.

"Susie is a busy girl these days," I start to probe.

"The Doernbecher fundraiser is coming up so there are a lot of meetings. She's very dedicated."

"Yeah, she is. Good charity too."

"Uh-huh," Jim stares at a steak.

"You want that one?"

"What?"

"The T-bone you're drooling on," I elbow him with a smile.

"Whatever, sure."

"Can I ask you something Jim?"

"Alright," he tenses.

"Do you ever get mad at Susie?"

"Mad?"

"Annoyed. Do you ever get fed up with how things are?"

"She's a lovely woman and I'm lucky to have her," he smiles. Poor sap looks like he means it too.

"Okay, yeah, I know, fine. We're all lucky. But answer my question: Do you ever get fed up with how things are?"

"What do you mean?"

I begin to get irritated with my buddy. Maybe he actually is a fucking robot. "Jim, work with me here, you go to work all day, everyday and she's running around all over town pretending to be the Princess of Portland."

His face contorts, "You mean her charity work?"

"Yeah, I know it's charity work, but, come on, half of those meetings are like happy hour, dude. They're just hanging out and you're home babysitting after a long day of doing whatever engineers do."

"I enjoy spending time with my kids."

"That's not the point, Jimbo. Were talking about you and your needs, when's the last time you went to see the

Grateful Dead?"

"Jerry Garcia's passed on," he reminds me.

"Okay, the Stones, Neil Young, the Who, whoever, you never used to miss the old war horses when they rolled through town."

"Susie was never much for concerts," he nods sadly.

"Okay, okay, good, that's my point dude. Who cares if she's into it – you're into it. When's the last time you did something you wanted to do?"

Jim shook his head, "I think you're looking at this all wrong. Marriage is a partnership, you give up things to be part of a team."

"Give up things? Do the math Spanky, you're the only one giving up things. Has Susie given up anything? Does she still play tennis at the club?"

"Yeah, but only three times a week."

"Does she go out with the girls?"

"Only for Thursday night Bunko."

"How many "charity" meetings and club functions a week does she attend?" I pressed.

"Three or four, I guess," he said.

"Three or four? Plus Bunko? Dude, you work all day and she's out every fucking night of the week? She parties more than a sorority bimbo, does that sound like a balanced and fair partnership to you? What is she sacrificing for you?"

"We still live on a cul-de-sac in Beaverton," he shrugs.

"Since when is living in a three thousand square foot house in a beautiful suburb a sacrifice?" I punched him on the arm. "You provide an excellent life for your family. You need to wake up and smell the coffee. She's got you turned so inside out it's embarrassing. When are you gonna stand up for yourself?"

I studied his passive face. The poor bastard didn't feel like he was getting a raw deal. His spirit has been broken so completely he doesn't even know he's a slave. He's happy to do the work and let her spend the money and dictate to him how to spend his time. He's happy to have a woman say she loves him as she's running out the door. His standards have been lowered so far that he doesn't even mind getting used and abused. I guess there could be peace of mind at the bottom of the well he's living in, but I doubt it. Maybe he can suppress his own desires until the kids are grown, maybe even until middle age, but I believe this is where the mythical "mid-life crisis" originates. A man sucks it up for as long as he can and then fucking snaps. He blows his retirement fund on a sports car (I recommend the Porsche C4 Cabriolet), drives to Vegas, gambles and bangs strippers for a couple weeks, runs out of money and slinks back home. The wife will deal with it because she's been calling the shots for decades and as long as her meal ticket returns to his work station, she's willing to forgive and forget. If he doesn't return, then get ready for the bloodiest divorce proceedings you can imagine. I guess it's a "win-win" situation for the housewives. Seems to me Jim is heading for a meltdown. Maybe he isn't even aware, but he's not the guy I met thirteen years ago. He's slowly receded into his own skin, becoming the servant his wife requires and in the process lost his individuality. He's mired in what I'll call the Big Pussy Stage.

"Is everything okay with you and Alicia?" His question surprised me.

"Why? What have you heard?"

"Susie and Alicia have been talking a lot lately, that's all."

"About me?"

"I think, some. I heard you bought her a new car," he grinned.

"So…what?"

"You're riding me about my business and you're kissing up to your wife by buying her a new car," he smirked.

This was my opening. Should I take it? Could this panty waste disguised as my old friend be trusted with the secret intelligence I had gathered or would he roll over and spill it to his boss lady?

"I, uh, okay here it is. This stays in the Circle of Trust." We both made an "okay" sign with our index finger and thumb – the official Circle of Trust hand signal. Jim brushes his hand along his knee and nonchalantly looks away. I also drop my signal below the waist, the sure sign of authenticity – a sacred promise is made.

"I bought the car to test a theory," I whispered. My voice barely rising above the sizzling steaks.

"What kind of theory?"

"I told her friends I wanted to buy her something and they laid out the make, model and serial number of the car Alicia wanted."

"So?"

"So? What's 'so?' "

"It's no mystery that the girls talk."

"Okay, right, I know. But Alicia had started a fight the night before to try and manipulate me into buying her a car."

"Wait, who manipulated you, Alicia or her friends?"

"You're not listening to me. I think that there is something going on here, in this neighborhood, that goes way beyond girlfriends gossiping with each other. There's some kind of organized effort on the part of the wives to...to...to get our money and make us do what they want," I sputtered.

"Yeah. It's called marriage," he shrugged.

"Jim, tell me you know what I'm talking about. Don't you sense it? Doesn't it feel like there's something going on that we just don't know about? I thought men were supposed to be the kings of their castles. I thought men were the hunters and gatherers. I thought men were supposed to be the brave and valiant knights defending their fair maidens from black knights and dragons and shit. Look at us man. What the hell, Jim? Does this seem right? When it's quiet at night do you even feel like you?" My voice trembled. "Jim, I went to the video store today and rented 'The Wedding Planner'."

"How's J-Lo in that?"

The more I tried to explain the crazier I sounded, Jim was in deep, deep denial. I would find no ally this day. "Not too good. But it's not all her fault, pairing her with Matthew what's-his-name was a mistake. He was awesome in 'Frailty,' but there was no chemistry with J-Lo at all."

Alicia rolled out with a tray of condiments for the burgers.

"How we doing boys?" she inquired with a smile.

"Great honey, almost ready here," I replied.

Susie brought out a big bowl of potato salad that smelled delicious.

"Jim, why don't you call the kids," she said.

"Yes, dear," he smiled.

The steaks were delicious, the conversation was light, kids frolicked around us and yet, I felt totally alone. Was Jim so far gone that he really had no idea what I was talking about? Maybe my words would sink in and Jim would come out of his coma someday.

I will say that Susie's potato salad was great. Need to get that recipe from her and right after that I'll swallow my hunting rifle.

August 11, 2003

Still no sex since buying Alicia her Mercedes. It's been a full week and nothing. Although I've been back in the marital bed for four days, I'm beginning to think I've been cut off. Yes, I'm afraid the Stay at Home Wife doomsday weapon has been deployed. It's an odd concept really, how can women control their men simply by cutting them off from sex? I don't know, but they sure do. They can't get us to do what they want by threatening physical violence – men are bigger and stronger, but still they have this crazy power over us. They've got us jumping through hoops to try to stay out of "dutch with the missus." We don't contradict them in public when they're babbling like morons about foreign policy, we don't interrupt them when they're telling a story wrong, in point of fact, we bend over backwards to avoid confrontation with them because we don't want them to cut us off. Those of us who respect the vow of monogamy (and I hear there are a couple of us) are then stuck with very few options for sexual release. Those who don't respect it call us suckers – they may be right. And don't think the women don't know that. Since the time of Abraham, he of the seventy wives, the women somehow managed to drive a cultural shift limiting men to a single wife. Oh sure, the Euros have that whole courtesan thing to fall back on, but in the USA that shit don't fly, they've got us over a barrel, boys. Men like sex. Women know this and leverage us. Most men would fast for a week if it meant some mattress shattering sex at the end of that week. But there must be something more to their power than simply holding out on us. I'm beginning to think there is correlation between their ability to confuse and manipulate our minds with their "house-wife-speak" and cutting us off. Don't you find yourself more disoriented the more hard-up you get? There could easily be a connection between our sperm count and the effectiveness of their "mind control." Think of it like this: what is your state of mind after sex? It's like a fresh rain has washed the filth from streets and the air is clean and cool. Speaking for myself, I'm never more clear headed as I am after a good pipe cleaning. All seems right with the world. I can see for miles.

On the other hand, when my "water pressure" has been building up for a week or two, I'm the most muddle-headed twit you'll ever come across. You could ask me, "Jim Brown, Barry Sanders or Gale Sayers, who is the greatest running back in NFL history?" and I won't be able to make a case for any of them. The only thing in my head right now is, "How many football players are named Gale?" and "Was Jim Brown in 'Kelly's Heroes' or 'The Dirty Dozen'? Normally, I could talk football with you all day, but right now my pocket rocket is tied in knots and I'm as ignorant and useless as a straight guy in an art gallery.

I've heard the old clichés that chicks are more interest-ed in sex before marriage because they're trying to hook the guy. Then after marriage, there's not much interest, you start hearing all about headaches and "I'm not in the mood" and all that. Seems like those clichés are based on fact. Seems to me once the chick snags you, she slacks off. I mean, guys can still get in the mood at the drop of a hat – this despite years of getting our chops busted and maybe the missus has put on a couple of pounds or something. Hell, if we've been wandering in the desert long enough, certain word combinations will get us hard as a brick bat: "I've always wanted to drive to China" or "Bend over and pick that up." Men are ready to throw down anytime, anywhere. We're men, it's what we do.

I guess I don't understand the housewife mindset, if it were me staying home everyday doing whatever I wanted, I'd be itching to jump my provider's bones every time she came home from work. I'd meet her at the door every night ready to give her a high, hard thank you. I can't think of a greater aphrodisiac than a person keeping me living in high cotton with nary a care – but that's me.

So here's what this whole deal seems to be shaping up like: if I were to stay single, I'd get to have tons of sex with a bunch of hot babes who are trying to land me as their sugar daddy. But I decided to get married and split my dough fifty-fifty and get sex only when my wife feels like it or, as I'm learning, wants something from me. And the fifty-fifty thing is a joke anyway, probably works out more like eighty-twenty – she gets that extra thirty percent bonus for looking good and keeping track of the kids – it's there in the small print. In the event of divorce, that figure is probably more like ten percent, because when the kids are visiting me in my three hundred square foot apartment they're going to want me to buy them toys and clothes and shit to prove I still love them. If marriage isn't a true partnership it can be one raw fucking deal.

The Bible talks about wives being submissive to their husbands. The wives are supposed to let their men be the leaders of the house and all that. I know the women's libbers went crazy over that one but they never finished reading the passage. It goes on to say that the men are supposed to love their wives like Christ loved the church. It doesn't say submit yourself to some abusive lunk head, what it means, I think, is let him be a man and he'll treat you right and take care of your needs and adore you. It's a give and take thing. You can't smash his nuts in a Creative Memories album, lock his bruised balls in the attic and expect him to sacrifice himself for you. You can't make him do that. If women adored their husbands and respected them and let them do the hunting and gathering and dragon slaying, they'd worship their wives the way they want to be worshiped. Now, I'm sure there have been plenty of guys down the line who let the deal go bad by not adoring and taking care of their wives and so on, but the theory is still right. My man Jim is doing the deal, but his wife ain't playing fair. Bottom line: somebody changed the rules on us – this wasn't the deal most of us made. Partners serving each other, cool, that's a deal founded on love. But this concept of us paying for them to be with us? This is starting to feel like the world's most expensive table dance.

It's almost midnight, the kids are asleep and I should be on my wife drilling for oil right about now. Weak moment, I admit. But right now, I'd do almost anything to be "un-cut off" and that is how they get you, I know. But I don't care. I miss Alicia. I wish I didn't know what I know. Maybe the housewives can hypnotize me, wipe my mind clean like they did in "Men In Black." One flash of light and I'll forget that all the housewives in my neighborhood are unified in a battle against their very own husbands. I want to forget that these housewives are following a cynical blueprint to take anything they want from us. How can we give them the world when they're so busy taking it?

August 12, 2003

Starting to lose my mind around the house. Alicia was preparing to pummel me with another mind numbing "Honey Do" list when my buddy, Doctor Robert, called begging me to join his foursome at some charity golf event. Somebody bailed on him at the last minute and he needed a fourth. I played the "it's for charity" card with Alicia and she seemed to go for it. She was probably glad to have me out of the house anyway, it has to be exhausting for her, putting up a front all the time.

I ride out to Quail Valley with Doctor Robert, who, while being a good dude is a very fucking odd duck. He's had a family practice for a couple decades and has been frugal with his money so he's basically set for life. He bought a sixty-foot yacht a couple years ago and we go fishing in Mexico on it every summer. He never catches anything, but I think he has a great time just hanging with the fellas. Doctor Robert always strikes me as the tag-a-long little brother, the last kid picked for teams on the playground – this despite the fact that many of the adventures we go on are at his invitation.

He's been married to this cute little woman named Jill for a bunch of years now. She's petite and reminds me of a gymnast or something. She has one of those tight little yoga bodies, a Dorothy Hamill haircut and a permanent smile – there was nothing not to like about Jill. But because she was always very polite to us boys, strangely respectful you might say, I've always been suspicious of her. Not many wives bother with the Eddie Haskell routine, you know? But maybe she's sincere, I don't know. Maybe it's one of those "any friend of my husband is a friend of mine" deals. There is never any judgement or sideways insults when I come around – she never even complained about my cigars. Maybe it's because she's a Mormon. I guess that's part of the drill, being the perfect subservient wife. I'm not sure what the magic white salamanders told Joseph Smith about housewives, but Doctor Robert's wife appears to be going along with the program. Jill lets this guy do whatever he wants, takes care of the kids and the house and all is good with the world. The Good Doctor also says the missus is no slouch in the sack. From the sound of it, he's hitting it three or four times a week and if he's too tired to ride her, she goes down on him without making a fuss. Amazing. The dude claims to have been blown six times this month alone. Be honest, how many years would you have to count back to total six blow jobs? Six years? Ten? He's probably full of shit, but it makes for a good story. Interestingly, though, all the other women in the neighborhood hate her – so maybe it is true. She's the damn rebel of the hood, making the other housewives look like cold fish.

Doctor Robert adores her, provides for her and she lets him be the man – the ancient formula is working. And apparently the little housewife conspiracy has been unable to crack the Mormon code, they can't find a way to recruit her. Must be like having a factory worker refuse to join the union, cross the picket line and then turn out to be the best employee the company has ever seen. The housewife "union bosses" must be thinking about burying her next to Jimmy Hoffa.

Of course, because she is a Mormon there is a trade off. In exchange for all that good head, Doctor Robert has to listen to replicants preach sermons about preparing to leave on the spaceship to take them wherever it is they're going to. And I suppose his wife wears those funny pajamas or underpants with a lock on them or whatever it is, but hey, if she strips down and goes bareback, I wouldn't much care what she sleeps in afterwards.

We arrive at the golf course and make our way to the registration tent. There, to my surprise, I see Larry and Jim hanging out, waiting for us. That's the thing with Doctor Robert, we don't really trust him because he's always messing with us.

I had asked him, "Who are we playing with today?"

"Couple of guys, good guys, you'll like 'em," he replied.

A couple of guys? Jim is a buddy and Larry, shit, he was my college roommate and is probably my oldest friend. A couple of guys? This calls for an eyebrow raise, Doctor Robert is up to something.

I hadn't played a round of golf with Larry since I sold my company earlier this summer. Occasionally, he'll invite me along if he's playing with some sports celebrity for work. Larry is in Sports Marketing at Nike so when Neil Lomax does his charity golf tournament or Peter Jacobsen is doing his tourney the place is always flooded with sports stars, past and present. I owe Larry for life for including me in a foursome with Charles Barkley. I've never laughed so hard in my life – the Round Mound of Rebound called me "Cracker" all day and I wore that moniker proudly, let me tell you.

Larry puts in the serious hours out at Camp Nike. Fair bit of travel too, but often to cool sporting events where he mingles with that elite class of men who seem to be above the suffocating grip of the housewife. I know those trips are Larry's only moments of relief, because his wife Kristen flat out owns him. She keeps him whipping it long and hard at the office so he'll earn bonuses and promotions to pay for cars and trips that she's already bought.

I knew Larry was in bad shape last spring when a few of us were going to Cabo on Doctor Robert's boat to fish and Larry said he "didn't want to go." I could understand if he "couldn't go." Or if he was "too busy" to go. But "didn't want" to go? Bullshit. He was too tired to fight. He didn't want to bring the trip up to Kristen only to have it shoved back down his throat. Larry was going under and there was nothing I could do about it. Watching him slide into the quicksand had been slow and painful. His wife and Alicia were best friends, so we spent a fair bit of time together, but Kristen seemed to make a habit of flaunting her power over him in front of me.

Larry and Kristen began dating at the U of O. From the beginning I thought she was wrong for him, but she played him perfectly. Just the right blend of holding out and giving in, she delivered that lethal combo of affection and aloofness. She made him crazy right from the beginning and got him thinking that he was going to lose her. Larry and Kristen got engaged in the fall of our senior year and that was the end of college for Larry. Soon my beer-bonging buddy was shopping at Bed, Bath and Beyond on Saturday nights. Sad. How the mighty have fallen. There were many Saturday nights where I consoled Lisa Caudill, the previously mentioned "most amazing woman in the history of college women," who had a crush on Larry. He went out with Lisa for a couple months before Kristen set her sights on him. I still don't know why Larry chose Kristen over Lisa. And try as I might, I myself was unable to steer my tenuous relationship with Lisa from that as "confidant/best friend of the former boyfriend" to anything romantic. She was too hurt and I was too young, dumb and stupid to know what to do. We both lost track of her after college, but she crosses my mind occasionally. I'm sure Lisa still flits across Larry's mind – the bastard actually saw what Lisa had under that amazing sweater.

After college, after I got married, our wives became friends and things became easier. There wasn't any tension with Kristen – she had won Larry and she knew there was nothing I could do about it. As we both had kids, Larry and I coached together and could steal "guy time" under the guise of working out a game plan for the first grade soccer team. If you've ever seen little kids play soccer, you know what an obvious ruse our coaching sessions actually were. Looking back I'm sure the wives knew all along. Embarrassing, we're no challenge for them at all. Recently, the indignities for Larry have mounted. His twelve year old kid Ron, who is blessed with unbelievable genetics, has grown to be nearly five foot ten and weighs a hundred thirty five pounds. He's a total stud athlete who, so far, has been relegated to the candy ass, Euro art fag sport of soccer. Hey, don't get me wrong, that sport is fine when the kids are little and all they want is to run around in the grass with their friends and eat orange wedges. But Ron is a full on stud – he should be playing an American sport like football. His father played college football for crying out loud. Sure he was a third stringer, but he did get in during garbage time of a blowout win over Stanford his junior season. Let me tell you, there was much drinking that night and multiple sorority babes were groped.

Anyway, Larry begs Kristen to let Ron play football, she puts on like she's considering it and then slams the door on them. She said it was too dangerous. Yeah it's dangerous, but not for the kids like Ron. Ron is the kid that makes it dangerous for all the little pee wee kids. This was a humiliating defeat for Larry. Ron was really counting on him and Larry couldn't close the deal. This conflict with Kristen seemed to be the decisive battle in the war and the real Larry is now laying in a bunker somewhere bleeding out – for the past nine months or so, he just hasn't seemed himself. It's a humbling thing to have your wife parade your nut sack around in front of your first born.

"Larry, you big dumb son-of-a-bitch, what are you doing here?" I hugged him.

"Golf, Beer and Babes. It's all I need."

"Kristen let you out to play golf?"

"Hell, no, she thinks I'm at work. And you better fucking play fast I have to be home by seven. If you knock an entire sleeve of balls into the water hazards like you did in Sunriver then I'm a dead man. You hold my life in your driver," he laughed.

Jim stepped up with his quick engineer wit, "You suck Mike." Yeah, they really know how to cut loose at Intel.

"Yes, golf, beer and BABES, this is a day that will go down in infamy," laughed Doctor Robert.

Babes? What's with the "babes" all of a sudden? Well, we made our way to the golf carts and I was met by a tan, beautiful young woman with enormous pink nipples attached to her enormous natural breasts. She wore an itty, bitty g-string, but, uh, yeah, she was pretty much bare butt ass naked.

"Hello there," I smiled.

"May I take your clubs for you?" she purred.

"Certainly you may," I handed her my bag and turned to my host. "Doctor?"

"Yeah?"

"Wondering who the naked chick is."

"Think she said her name is Amaretto," he replied.

"Amaretto?" I repeated. I looked around at the fellas who were enjoying this prank way too much.

"She's your caddy," he snickered.

"My caddy? She know anything about golf?"

"Who cares? Look at that rack," the Good Doctor howled.

He had a good point there. But at the risk of sounding stupid, I asked the obvious.

"Uh, so, you know, uh, why the hell isn't she wearing anything?"

"She's a nude caddy."

"Oh, sure, a nude caddy. Are you gonna quit jacking me up or am I gonna have to kick your ass?" I turned to Amaretto, "I'm gonna need that seven iron."

Amaretto put a hand on her hip and shifted her weight – gravity did some very good things. The Good Doctor, Jim and Larry cracked up.

"Amaretto works at Stars Cabaret, they're sponsoring the tournament," Doctor Robert finally offered.

"You said this thing was a benefit for a women's shelter. That's what I told my wife."

Larry stepped up, "The strippers are giving all the money to the shelter."

"You could've mentioned this one little detail on the phone. 'Oh, by the way, naked strippers are going to carry your golf clubs for you.' " I was thinking of how this whole nude golf thing was going to play with Alicia. I really didn't need any bad PR right now. Even though I could legitimately plead ignorance, you know she'd bust my chops over this.

Jim was making an ass of himself drooling over my caddy. "This is gonna be awesome."

"Hey, Holcomb, get your own fucking naked caddy," I snapped.

Amaretto, for her part, was looking a little bored, which speaks volumes about the exotic entertainment industry. She's naked on a golf course, getting gawked at by a foursome of domesticated executives and she's yawning and casually pulling the g-string out of her crack – what other profession prepares you for such a scenario?

"We're supposed to put a single in her g-string on each hole and buy her a ten dollar Coke on the front nine and another one on the back nine," Larry said.

"I suppose I'll have to tip extra each time she bends over to get the ball out of cup." Damn I'm funny. The picture slowly materialized in their feeble brains.

Jim and Larry exchanged a high five, "Oh, yeah. This is gonna be awesome." Shut up you fucking nerds, what are you, fifty?

"Before this goes any further, I want this entered into the Circle of Trust," I said. Jim, Larry and I dropped our hands below our waist and gave the signal. The Good Doctor waved his hand around and peered through the "circle" at us, a bad sign that I regrettably chose to ignore.

I slipped into the cart next to Amaretto.

"Amaretto? That's your real name, huh?" She just winked and slammed down the accelerator pedal with a six-inch high heel. I was thrown back, banged my head off the inside of the cab and clung to the seat to keep from falling from the cart. I swear she topped thirty-five miles per hour. I'll bet my vixen of the links had tampered with the cart's speed governor.

The first few holes were amazing. This naked girl caddy thing is pretty genius, not because of the titillation of bare flesh but because I was so distracted from the golf that I was hitting the my tee shots like John Daly and putting like Vijay Singh. I managed to keep a straight face as Amaretto and her twins would bounce up to me with a suggestion.

"You've been slicing your five iron, maybe you want to bust out the fairway driver and see if you can hit it straight?" she smiled.

I nodded compliantly, calmly, but my brain was saying "Don't stare at her ass. Don't stare at her ass. Don't stare at her ass." Then I proceed to drop the shot six feet from the pin. When you're so completely rattled by the presence of a naked woman, you don't get fixated on the tiny details of golf. Remember, we're talking about a sinister, satanic game that can snap a man's soul in two. But today I was cruising, baby. I wonder if I can add Amaretto to my membership at Pumpkin Ridge – a few naked chicks patrolling the fairways is just what that place needs.

This benefit tournament not only gave me the opportunity to humiliate my associates with a devastating round of golf, but also the chance to pick the brain of a hottie who doesn't appear to be in league with the housewife mafia. Of course, if the housewives took to our neighborhood streets wearing nothing but a g-string all the men would surrender before sunset and happily become their slaves. A strategy for the housewives to consider, of course, we may already be their slaves and just not know it – that's what I'm trying to find out.

In point of fact, Amaretto was a pretty cool girl. I got in good with her by chatting her up without staring at her boobs. She knew I wanted to check her out, like everybody else, but she appreciated my restraint and the fact that I actually maintained eye contact most of the time. I spoke as casually as if I was discussing life insurance policies with my State Farm agent. Note to my State Farm agent, if she went topless I'd probably be in the office every couple of weeks adding riders to my homeowner's policies.

As it turns out, Amaretto was in the nursing program at Portland State. Dancing was the best paying job she could find and working nights allowed her to carry a full class load during the day. I know, a nursing student working her way through school as a stripper – haven't we seen this ABC Afterschool Special before? Well, clichés become clichés because they're true more often than not.

"What are you going to do after college?"

"Go into nursing. I thought you were listening," she sniffed.

"I thought that whole 'I'm a college student/stripper' thing was a line they teach you at the club"?

"No, I'm actually going to be a nurse."

"Don't you want to get married?"

"Are you proposing?"

"Funny, I like that. No, but, I mean, nursing is a difficult profession and it doesn't pay that much," I explained.

"It pays alright. Besides, I want to help people, take care of them when they're hurting. I think I'd be good at that," she shrugged.

I went for the gold, trying to crack her shield of politically perfect answers, "But couldn't you snag one of those VP types who come into your joint? You'd be set for life and never have to work for it."

She considered the question for a moment. Despite her overdone make up I noticed how beautiful she was, her hair blowing in the breeze as we drove up to the next tee. "I don't know. Maybe if I fell in love I'd feel differently. But if you don't love the guy it'd be hard work – harder work than nursing."

"Good answer. But you have to be the exception to the rule, right? Most of the girls are hunting for sugar daddies, right?" I probed.

"Nah, most of the girls at the club are young, they love the freedom the money gives them. That's enough for now. And if you're trying to say we need a man to be happy, that's a load of arrogant shit. Maybe when I'm older I'll feel differently, but I want to see what the world holds for me before I get chained to some guy. No offense." She handed me the nine iron.

I handed back the club, "I usually go with a seven iron at this distance."

"This hole is only a one hundred eighty yard, par three. You're not a pussy are you?" Good sense of humor this girl has. Her boobs jiggled as she laughed, I did my best not to stare. I took the nine iron and hit a rainmaker that nearly made me weep. The high arc on the ball was textbook perfect – it bit on the tight green and rolled to within a foot of the cup. I had never hit a wedge that well in my life.

"No, you're not a pussy," she grinned. I handed her the club and turned to the cart and her strong, little hand grabbed my ass. Should I tip extra for that? I'm happy to, believe me.

What I was trying to figure out was, when did these spunky young single women like Amaretto or the missing barista, go over to the other side? When do they go to the dark side and become Volvo Driving Soccer Moms? Do they burn out in the work world? Do they wake up one day and decide they want to be pampered? Or are they recruited, like in the armed forces and Mary Kay?

"I don't suppose you get many suburban mom types coming down to see your gymnastics on the brass pole, do you?"

"Once in a while. They're funny. They watch you like hawks, like they're trying to pick up new moves to keep their husbands from getting bored," she said.

"If only that were true," I mumbled to myself.

"Sometimes a guy will come in with his wife and the woman will be having a great time, but the dude is a nervous wreck, totally losing his mind. She's talking to all the girls, tipping every song and all that. He's sitting there sucking his Coke through the little stirring straw, trying to avoid looking at any naughty parts. Weird."

"That would be strange to take my wife to Stars on a date. I'd go hoarse yelling over the music, 'No honey, you look better than her and her. Yes, you even look better than that 21 year old with the perfect tan and tiny waist. No, I'm not just saying that. Besides, those boobs are probably fake anyway." She laughs. I love Amaretto's laugh, or maybe it's the jiggling that accompanies the laugh. Either way, the laughing is a good thing.

"Sandi," she says after she stops laughing.

"Sandi?"

"My real name is Sandi," she smiled a nice, real, honest, genuine smile.

I muster all the mock shock I can, "Are you saying Amaretto is a…is a…is a stage name?" She punches me playfully on the arm. "I can't believe you lied to me. What

141

do we have if we can't be honest with each other?" I grinned.

At the end of the round I unrolled a pile of bills to donate to the charity and I slipped Sandi a Benjamin and whispered in her ear, "That's for you." She got up on her toes, her perfect, soft chest squishing against me, and gave me a kiss – her tongue darted in and out of my mouth. I about had a heart attack.

"Come by the club sometime," she winked.

Hanging out with Sandi/Amaretto had made me feel better for some reason. I guess I was intoxicated by her flirtatious attentions, Lord knows my male ego had taken a few hits in recent weeks, but deep down I guess I was relieved that the neighborhood housewife syndicate has not been able to corrupt the fine exotic dancers/college students in our community. There was still a refuge for the men. Oh sure, I'd paid this young lady a few hundred dollars to hang out and flirt today – but as I was learning, there may be little or no difference between Amaretto and the two-faced housewives in my cul-de-sac. Oh, maybe there is one distinction to be drawn: at least Amaretto tells you up front it's a "pay for play" deal. All the poor husbands on my street have been working under the assumption that their wives love them and are devoted to them. Suckers.

I update my scorecard: the housewives haven't been able to get to the Mormons or the Strippers. Hey, that could be a reality show – Mormon Strippers versus Soccer Moms.

August 13, 2003

Alicia commented on my good spirits this morning.

"I shot a great round of golf yesterday. I was unconscious. And, uh, I missed you and am glad to be home today."

Truth be told, Amaretto was on my mind. Every time I think of her I sport wood. I'm amazed I didn't walk around with a tent in my pants yesterday.

I call Doctor Robert to thank him for including me in the foursome. Funny, I barely saw those guys yesterday. Amaretto, uh, Sandi and I were always at least a hundred yards in front of those hacks. I took honors on every hole but one. And even when we were standing around in the tee box together, I was so mesmerized by Sandi that I don't even remember talking to them.

August 14, 2003

Took the kids to the pool today so Alicia could return a dress to Saks Fifth Avenue. I splashed around with the little monkey bastards for a while until Timmy left scratches on my back so deep that they actually bled. Great, I'm sure someday soon I'll be explaining to Alicia that the scratches came from her son and not in the heat of passion. Who clips this feral child's nails anyway? Don't I pay for a nanny? Cassie reminds me that Cynda, our nanny, doesn't come back to stay with us until school starts.

We stayed late into the day at the pool then things started to turn weird. As usual, I was trying to spy on the housewife contingent that have set up shop on the sun deck adjacent the Social Pool. All seemed quiet and normal most of the day and I stayed close to the pool, opting to stay out of their telepathic range. I didn't need an "eye headache" and didn't want to be "hypnotized" and be rendered a drooling, unconscious blob again. More than anything I was afraid that this coven was capable of some form of mind scan and would pick up on my constant thoughts of Sandi the stripper. Funny how one French kiss from a nude caddy can do that to your brain. Scrambled man, scrambled.

Anyway, as the sun dropped behind the West Hills, I noticed the housewives begin to grow agitated. Instead of lounging about chatting and reading magazines, they were now sitting up or standing. I guess they were getting ready to leave but didn't really seem to want to go home. The bliss of sunbathing was over and they had to leave this cocoon and return to real life. Maybe they were having trouble with their husbands or remembered an unpaid parking ticket or had suddenly grown concerned about North Korea's nuclear capability. Whatever it was, their moods had done a one-eighty.

The housewives began to pair off. Pretty soon each of these couples were engaged in very animated, contentious conversations. "What do they have to be mad about?" I thought. From a distance they almost looked like football players pairing off before a game to fire each other up. Yelling, talking smack, banging each other's shoulder pads, getting up in each other's grills, yanking their face masks – these women were getting each other all jacked up. If this is what went on in the woods at midnight in eighteenth century New England you could hardly blame the townsfolk for putting the torch to 'em.

I walked an arm load of wet towels over to a basket and lingered, trying to eavesdrop on the housewives.

"Have you gained weight?" Debra squinted.

"Those fake fingernails make you look like a whore," Kristen retorted.

"Those new flats you bought make your feet look stumpy," I heard Melanie say.

"Did an entire hornet's nest sting your lips?" laughed Busty Red.

"Who's talking, you walking Botox disaster. Can you even close your eyes at night?" Melinda shot back.

The insults were personal, hideous and coming so fast I couldn't even keep up.

"If you were seven feet tall and weighed three hundred pounds your new boobs would almost be in proportion,"

Melinda countered.

"At least I have something for the gardener to stare at Miss-I'm-Allergic-to-Silicon," spat Busty Red.

Their eyes blazed brighter with each stinging put down, but they stood right in there and took the punishment. Each woman slamming the other and just as they reached a fever pitch, they turned to the children.

I retreated into the water as they summoned their kids. Peering over the edge of the pool, I watched as these she-goblins rounded up their respective offspring. Kids hesitantly crawled from the pool to receive their towel and an unprovoked tongue-lashing. The first couple of families left – the mom at the end of her rope, the children crying and upset. Then the next group, identical. Like it was some kind of ritual, a pagan ceremony of familial distress and upset. Why end a perfectly relaxing day like that?

"Glad they're not coming home to my house," I found myself thinking. Then it hit me like a diamond bullet. That's exactly what these women were up to: they were cranking it up to blast their husbands when they got home.

"How was your day honey?" the poor sap would ask.

"Oh my God! Don't get me started," she would shriek.

"Maybe we could go out to dinner?" the poor sap would hear himself mumbling.

"I'm a little tired, but sure. That's a good idea." Then she'll walk up to her bedroom to change and cackle like a cartoon super villain.

The fact is these women spent a perfectly lovely day kicking it by the pool with all their best pals while their kids were being baby sat by the lifeguard. But if their husbands were to find out how easy and stress free their gig actually is they'd lose their leverage at home. So these women wind up their kids to the point of tears and the housewives work each other into some kind of estrogen frenzy. No mortal man is prepared for the tornado of emotions that is lying in wait for him. At the end of his stressful day is an ambush. The calculating housewife probably even pinches the kids right before he opens the door and – she bang – Mr. Hardworking Provider is fighting for his life. Instead of thinking, "it's good to be home after a challenging day of earning dough for my family," he's thinking, "Damn, I thought getting reamed by my district manager all day, without the common courtesy of a reach around, was tough – but my wife has it worse. I guess I have the easy job and I'm never going to that frigging pool again."

Is everything a ruse with these women? Did it ever occur to them that we might actually like the idea that they were having a nice day at the pool? It's in our nature to be sacrificing at work to make a better life for our loved ones, it actually fuels us. We're proud to bring home a paycheck and have our wife spend it all. Taking care of our people makes us feel like men. If our wives admitted that they are lounging in the lap of luxury, they could probably get us to work even harder – because it would feel to us like it was all worth it. You know men are prone to a good martyr complex. Where do you think the "I'm hit, go on without me, I'll hold them as long as I can" mentality comes from? But if we're slaving away and no one is benefiting, our morale slumps. What's the point, right? I'm miserable at work. No matter how well things go my wife isn't satisfied. What's the point? But knowing these women, they know that already too. I haven't figured this all out yet, but why are they intent on taking things from us that we'd willingly give? That's the part that's pissing me off.

August 15, 2003

The shit has hit the fan.

Alicia is up early preparing a three course breakfast. Unusual, but very welcome. She sets down a plate of hotcakes in front of me. "Would you like some syrup?"

"Sure."

"Who is Amaretto?" she asks nonchalantly.

What the fuck? My hair ignited and my mind flailed wildly in the quicksand of her question. Where did she hear about Amaretto? Okay, relax, calm down, nothing happened...except for one hot little French kiss. A kiss nobody knows about, idiot. Okay, be cool.

All of those thoughts fired off in about a tenth of a second. I finished chewing a bite and calmly answered, "She was the caddy at that golf tourney the other day."

"Don't you mean she's a stripper?"

"I guess that's what she does for work, yeah," I shrugged.

"Is that it?" Alicia stood with her hands on her hips.

"She was a pretty good caddy. I shot a seventy-seven."

"I hear that all she wore was a g-string and stilettos," Alicia smoldered.

"I guess you've heard it all then."

"She was pretty wasn't she?"

"Come on hon, she was my caddy."

"Did you enjoy her silver dollar nipples? I'll bet you did." She was spitting mad at this point. Which, I have to say, I found interesting. For the woman who has been playing me like a fiddle to be this upset...interesting...have I found a chink in the armor? Was she actually concerned that someone could steal her meal ticket? Or was she play acting this whole thing? Remember, she could actually be two moves ahead, even now. Is she that calculating? Like she's praying for infidelity or something so she can sue for divorce, get her dough and be rid of me? I don't know. She seems pretty steamed. Maybe her ego actually took a hit, hard to say for sure.

"Anything you'd like to say for yourself?" she hissed.

"It was a fundraiser. All the tips went to the women's shelter," I shrugged. Alicia stomped out of the room. "For the record, her nipples are more like Susan B. Anthony's," I muttered to myself.

Larry called from work to tell me that Doctor Robert had broken the Circle of Trust. Big surprise, that fuckstick had set us up. He invites us to a golf tourney with strippers, hires one for me and then goes home and tells his sex slave-Mormon-wifey all about it. He probably has an arrangement with Jill: each time he drops dime on his buddies with some serious dirt, she rewards him by slipping into a rubber bondage suit or something.

Apparently, Jill, with motive and opportunity, ran into our wives at the Pioneer Place mall and all too happily spilled the story of the nude golf tournament. Judging by the steam coming out of Alicia's ears, Jill didn't skimp on the details. Jill probably mentioned the high heels that made Amaretto's calves sleek and taut, she probably mentioned the g-string that framed her tight butt and, of course, we already have confirmation she mentioned those now famous silver dollar nipples. Nice going Jill, you freak. Why would you tell the other wives? What was the point of narcing us out? Was it some weird game of "I'm a more understanding wife than you? My hubby can go hang out with strippers and I don't mind, because I trust him and he'll always come home to me." Was Jill trying to justify her subservient wife act to the other wives? Maybe she was trying to convert them? "I give him everything and he tells me everything. Can you say the same?" Jill knows the other wives can't say that.

So anyway, Larry is in the dog house big time and I assume I'm headed for another night of marital bliss alone on my couch. Thank God for the Beast.

Larry was bummed, but not that bummed. "I'm already twenty thousand points in the hole anyhow."

What's with the points? I remember overhearing some of the housewives, including his wife Kristen, talking about the points.

"Twenty thousand points?" I repeated.

"Oh yeah, I'm down for the count. I'll be in diapers again before I'm back to scratch – unless I shoot Kristen's deadbeat dad or take her to the diamond mines in Sierra Leone."

"Back up. What's with the points?"

"The points?"

"Yeah, you said points." Am I speaking Spanglish here?

"Yeah. Points. As in the Point System," now he was the one sounding exasperated.

"Slow down, the Point System?"

"You've never heard of the Point System? It's like one of those laws of thermodynamics: for every action there is an equal and opposite reaction. Every thing you do that your wife finds favor with adds points, everything you do that pisses her off – subtracts points," Larry explained.

"And it's actually a system. A formal, agreed upon standard?" This was starting to explain a lot of things.

"Yeah, I guess. I mean, I didn't really agree to it. It's like gravity I guess, you can disagree with it but that doesn't change things," he said.

"Where did you hear about it? Who told you?" I pressed him.

"Well, nobody. I sorta just figured it out. I've been married a long time man."

This is how the women have lapped us. They talk. They share their experiences with each other. They trade industry secrets. Men talk about football and some chick in tight jeans they saw pumping gas over on Burnside Street. No wonder we're getting our asses kicked.

"You never mentioned it to me," I said, an edge rising into my voice. "I'm you're best friend since we're eighteen and you don't tell me about the Point System?"

"Settle dude. I figured you knew about it. You've been married longer than me."

The phone clicked.

"Hello?"

"Yeah, I'm still here," Larry said.

"Did you hear that?"

"Hear what?"

The phone clicked again.

"That. Was that a click? Did you hear it this time?" I was starting to freak.

"No. I don't know. I guess," Larry mumbled.

"Are you calling from your office?" I asked.

"No, I'm on my cell."

"You're calling me on a cell phone?" I screamed.

"Don't worry. I have like five thousand free minutes."

"Hang up now. Hang up. I'll talk to you later," I slammed down the phone.

Now, I'm not trying to be paranoid but I definitely heard that phone click, I know I did. Now personally, I don't know how to tap a phone, but that was the first thought that crossed my mind. Someone had tapped my phone or Larry's phone. Was someone listening in on our conversation? Who? Alicia? Does she know how to tap phones? Maybe Kristen knows how. Maybe the grand poo-bah of the neighborhood housewife coalition did it. Had they heard Larry spill the beans about the point system?

August 16, 2003

Been up working on this Point System thing. I feel like an idiot. How could I not have seen this before? If you assume a Point System, then things become less random, less based on a woman's mood. There is an equal and opposite reaction to any force in a relationship. It's so clear to me now. I haven't quite worked out a value system that makes total sense, and I suspect it's some kind of sliding scale anyway, probably different for each relationship. That's probably why more men haven't come together and said, "Hey this Point System thing sucks" – the house-wives have cleverly disguised it. As best as I can figure, the Point System is loosely based on the airline industry frequent flier system in that the values randomly shift from time to time, just to keep us off balance. One week twenty thousand miles gets you a free coach ticket, the next week it gets you a bag of peanuts and you need fifty thousand miles just to upgrade.

While there are few things you can do to earn points, the Point System is mostly about you losing points and being in debt to the missus.

THE POINT SYSTEM

Late To Pick A Kid Up After School   -500 POINTS

(If you forget the kid altogether and the wife has to go get him/her, subtract another 500 points.)

Surprise Your Wife With Flowers   +25 POINTS

(If you "overpay" for the bouquet at a gourmet grocery store or bring the flowers home in an expensive vase that your wife "doesn't have room for in the cupboard," lose 20 points.)

Disagree With Your Wife In Public   -1,000 POINTS

(If, after your company has left, you try to explain to your wife that she misinterpreted your harmless comment, subtract another 500 points, arguers never prosper.)

**Apologizing To Your Wife For Disagreeing
With Her In Public   +1 POINT**

(Again, quickly surrender, without trying to justify your point or risk being docked another 500 points.)

Boys Night Out   -2,500 POINTS

(This includes, but is not limited to, rock concerts, taking in a ball game, skiing, racquetball, softball or dinner. Introduce alcohol in any form and instantly subtract another twenty five hundred points. Introduce any activity that makes your clothes smoky, involves a night club hand stamp, the smell of women's perfume or nude caddies, subtract another five thousand points.)

Clean Out Garage Without Being Asked   +10 POINTS

(This includes moving boxes up to the crawl space, sweeping out the entire garage and removing the rotten food from the extra freezer that broke down earlier in the summer. Be sure that you don't suggest that your wife is a "pack rat" or suggest renting a dumpster so you "can throw some of this crap out" or you'll be docked 500 points.)

Forget The Anniversary Of The Day
You And Your Wife First Met   -1,000 POINTS

(Don't try to make up for this by remembering her birthday, the anniversary of your first date, the anniversary of your engagement, the anniversary of your actual wedding day or the birthdays of any or all of your children or she'll dock you another 1,000 points).

Loan Your Brother-In-Law Money   +250 POINTS

(A tough exchange rate here. I loaned him a thousand dollars and, by my estimation, earned about five hundred points for it. Of course, the loan was later described as an "investment" in his fledgling Amway business. He never paid back the grand, but I do have 200 boxes of environmentally friendly SA8 laundry soap stacked in my garage. Refer to this "investment" as the "loan" that it was and get docked 500 points.)

Get Busted Looking At Another Woman -2,500 POINTS

(Who made this point system anyway? We get penalized for simple genetics? The busty waitress leans over our table and her cleavage stands up and salutes — of course, my eyes are going there. My wife's eyes went there too. But I get tagged for an

involuntary reaction? No fair. It's not like I was lusting after the waitress or something. I was looking, not gaping. Besides, my wife is always looking at men when we're out. I'll say, "Baywatch boy there is pretty hot, eh?" But she wriggles out with a comment like, "Oh, I didn't really notice, I was thinking you'd look nice in his blue jacket." Damn she's bullet proof. Get docked another thousand points for trying to bust her.)

Host Your Mother-In-Law For A Month +1,000 POINTS

(This can be a good way to score points. Yeah, a month is a long time, but if you always keep a smile on your face and stay in a state of semi-consciousness, you can really skate. The mom-in-law feels welcome and she totally keeps your wife occupied. If you're careful, you can get away with working late a few times a week. Just a note: actually stay late and work, don't go to a sports bar and come home with smoke in your clothes, you'll be docked 2,000 points.)

Here's the chilling thing about the Point System – every fucking thing you do has points attached to it. Sometimes that goes in your favor, but as you'll see on the following chart it mostly goes against you. I understand how Larry is 20,000 points in the hole.

THE POINT SYSTEM HANDY REFERENCE GUIDE
WAYS TO LOSE POINTS

Leaving The Toilet Seat Up	**-100 POINTS**
Leaving The Cap Off The Toothpaste	**-100 POINTS**
Leaving The Milk Out	**-100 POINTS**

Leaving Hair In The Bathroom
    Sink Or Tub   **-250 POINTS**

Watching A Discovery Channel Documentary On New
    Guinea And Your Wife Walks In And Won't Believe
    You That It's Not Soft Core Porn   **-250 POINTS**

Leaving Your Underwear On The Floor   **-250 POINTS**

(if underwear has skid marks)   *(-500 POINTS)*

Detonate In The Bathroom   **-500 POINTS**

(forget to spray deodorizer)   *(-750 POINTS)*

Driving Your Wife's Car And Not
    Returning The Seat To Her Position   **-500 POINTS**

Leaving Food To Rot Under The Bed
    After A Late Night Snacking Binge   **-750 POINTS**

Yawning While Your Wife Repeats
    Gossip From The Spa   **-750 POINTS**

Going To The Gym Directly From Work
    Without Calling Home To Say You'll Be
    Late For Dinner   **-1,000 POINTS**

Ruining A Family Vacation By
    Losing Your Temper   **-1,000 POINTS**

Getting Busted Watching The "Paris
    Hilton" Movie On The Internet   **-2,500 POINTS**

Hinting At Or Outright Suggesting Sex   **-2,500 POINTS**

Sulking About Not Getting Any Sex   **-5,000 POINTS**

WAYS TO EARN POINTS

Watch The News With Your Wife And Listen
    Intently To Her Assessment Of The Economy
    And/Or The Crisis In The Middle East   **+10 POINTS**

Driving Your Wife's Car And Returning It Clean And With A Full Tank Of Gasoline	+10 POINTS
Leaving Work To Attend A Child's Event	+10 POINTS
Doing The Dishes Without Being Asked	+25 POINTS
Send The Wife To A Spa Of Her Choosing	+25 POINTS
Babysitting The Kids After Work So Your Wife Can Go To Bunko With Her Friends	+25 POINTS
Watch 'Will & Grace' With Your Wife And Pretend To Enjoy It	+50 POINTS
Making Your Wife Breakfast In Bed	+50 POINTS
(if you made food she doesn't like)	*(+1 POINT)*
Taking Your Wife Out To The Movies	+50 POINTS
(if film stars Meg Ryan or Julia Roberts)	*(+100 POINTS)*
(if film stars Sean Penn or Michael Caine)	*(+1 POINT)*
Going Out To Dinner With A Couple Of Your Wife's Choosing	+100 POINTS
(if she argues with the other wife)	*(+1 POINT)*
Agree With Every Interior Design Decision Your Wife Makes During A Remodel	+100 POINTS
Take The Family On Vacation	+250 POINTS
Taking Your Wife On A Weekend To A Warm Weather Destination During The Rainy Oregon Winter	+250 POINTS
Spring For An Expensive Anniversary Ring	+1,000 POINTS
Buying Wife A Brand New Luxury Car	+5,000 POINTS

THINGS MEN SPEND THEIR POINTS ON

Ten Quiet Minutes To Read The Paper After Work Without Being Hassled By Kids	-500 POINTS

Picking The Movie On Date Night	-500 POINTS
Getting To Pick A Gangster Video At Blockbuster	-500 POINTS
Dining Out At Your Favorite Steak House	-1,000 POINTS
Sit On Your Ass And Watch College Football All Day	-1,000 POINTS
Hosting A Super Bowl Party For Your Friends	-1,000 POINTS
Getting To Decorate One Room In Your Own House	-2,500 POINTS
Permission To Buy A New Set Of Golf Clubs	-2,500 POINTS
Permission To Spring For Front Row Seats At Springsteen	-2,500 POINTS
Permission To Buy A Big Screen TV	-5,000 POINTS
Take A Fishing Trip To Mexico With The Fellas	-5,000 POINTS
Engaging In Barely Adequate, Married Person, "Appointment Sex"	-5,000 POINTS
Stay Over In Vegas For The Weekend After The Convention	-10,000 POINTS
Semi-Annual, Totally Unplanned, Exciting, Spontaneous Sex (with your Wife, ass clown)	-10,000 POINTS
Receiving Oral Sex	-10,000 POINTS

Those are just a few examples of the Point System at work. You can see what we're up against here. And keep in mind that these point awards can be changed on the whim of the housewife. Boys, the house is dealing from a stacked deck. We're trying, against all odds, to build up enough points with the missus so that she'll cut us some slack and give us back a chunk of our life. But it ain't gonna happen, ever. Why? You don't have enough points, and you never will.

This Point System is like a VISA card that charges 2,000% interest, compounded hourly. But who agreed to this system? At least when you order a credit card you have to sign a form. I never agreed to this Point System. Larry didn't agree. The old car collector didn't agree. Did you agree to this deal? So who did? Did some guy sell us out? Did some Judas dude cut a deal for more favorable terms and leave the rest of us dangling from the tree?

And why don't we keep track of their points? Because they're not on the Point System – we are. The wives are holding all the points. They are the presidents of their own banks, they print the money and drive the armored cars. This is starting to smell like Enron to me. Enron makes a deal, Arthur Andersen audits the deal to make sure everything is square. The problem is, Enron is paying Arthur Andersen to do the audit. If the deal goes down, Arthur Andersen makes a ton of green. If they shit can the transaction, they don't get to audit any more Enron deals. Why would Arthur Andersen drop dime on Enron? They wouldn't. They'd be biting the hand that feeds them. So the women here developed their point system and only housewives know about it and administer all the records – it's a perfect system.

But how could the housewife mafia have implemented this system against our will? Did they set it up when we weren't paying attention? And how do the housewives maintain this system? First, they nag or yell to create unwanted conflict. Two, they bombard us with "Honey Do" lists to occupy our time with mundane activities – if we resist, again, unwanted conflict. And, of course, women can cut us off from sex. This is their most effective tactic and their ability to go without sex for longer stretches than men gives them a distinct advantage. Once we've given them children they don't need us the way we need them. If only we knew. I've seen single women in their thirties start getting squirrely about having kids. I guess they hear their biological clock ticking. Well, whatever anxiety or stress they're feeling at that time, that itch they need to scratch – I feel it every morning when I wake up with a woody. I haven't even put my feet on the floor and I'm trying to figure out how I'm going to get laid that day. A man's "biological clock" is going off every damn day and women know it and use it against us.

August 17, 2003

Alicia is out at Bunko night with the girls. Instead of nodding and smiling like I always do I had the audacity to ask, "What is Bunko, exactly?"

"It's a game, sweetie. I'll be back by ten. Eleven at the latest," Alicia said as she scurried about the bedroom with one shoe on.

"Maybe we could play at home sometime," I said, making conversation.

"I don't know. Maybe."

"How do you play, anyway?" I probed.

"I'm going to be late."

"I mean, is it like poker? Do you play for money?"

"Sometimes, it's a hard game to explain," she said, brushing me off.

"Do you play with cards or dice?"

"Honey, Bunko is just something I do with the girls on Thursday, it's no big thing. If you don't want me to go, I won't go."

"No, it's not that. I was curious, that's all." I shrugged.

"I've been going to Bunko night for seven years, you've never asked me about it before." I felt a Jedi housewife mind scan coming.

"It's not against the law for a husband to worry about his wife," I backpedaled.

"Alright, I don't want you to worry. Usually there are ten or twelve of us. We rotate hosts, but Debra likes showing off her remodel so she's hosted every Thursday this month. We'll spend the first half-hour getting caught up and then, table coffee talk snack gyroscope elephant broccoli," she continued speaking in an earnest tone but suddenly her sentences were missing words.

I blinked hard, trying to follow her – damn, she was doing it to me again. I tried to listen. I tried to pay attention. But she had busted out the hypnotizing-Housewife-Navajo-Bushmen-Code Talk and the world began to blur.

"Sounds fun," I slurred, hoping she'd release me from the mind numbing conversation.

"See you later," I heard her say. I felt her lips touch my cheek.

The slam of the front door brought me back to reality. From now on I'll have to be less obvious when digging for information.

Went to the park with the kids while Alicia is at Bunko. The kids head straight for the playground, leaving me to watch all the unleashed, four legged crapping machines run loose. Do dog owners think all that shit magically disintegrates once their precious Fido runs away from the steaming pile?

I strike up a conversation with a sweet little blue hair watching her three little darlings, let's call her Grams. I catch her staring down her nose at some cute mom pushing her infant around in a baby jogger. The super stroller had more options on it than my Porsche.

"I don't know how these women today get away with it," she muttered.

"Get away with it?" I heard myself say. Grams looked me over.

"Your wife at Bunko?" she asked. My jaw dropped.

"Uh, yeah, as a matter of fact she is."

"Then you probably know what I mean. You spent the day providing for your family and she's the one out for the evening?" She started to cough, I was about to perform the Heimlich when I realized she was coughing "Bullshit."

"Things have changed since your day, huh?" I prompted.

"Uh, yeah, a tad bit, I'd say," she said sarcastically. "My daughter married a nice young man, a lawyer. They have these three beauties together then she up and divorces him. And who has to pick up the slack? Me. Don't get me wrong, I love this time with my grand babies and I love my daughter, but she got some bad advice."

"Irreconcilable Differences?" I asked.

"More like 'hit and run.' My son-in-law never knew what hit him, poor sap. No respect for the old ways – that's what it was. If a husband is willing to bust his britches at work so a woman can be home raising those kids, well, that's a system that works. It's a blessing to have that time with your kids, it goes fast, let me tell you. And the men are missing out on a lot going to the office and dealing with all that business. But that's his part and if he does his part, the wife is obligated to do hers. It's a partnership you know. That's how it was with me and Elvin, God rest his soul."

"You must have felt cooped up, being in the house all day," I studied her face.

"I said it was a blessing. Aren't you listening?"

"Sorry, I thought maybe –"

"That's propaganda. 'Cooped up in the house, doing chores'. That's what they tell the girls these days. Like it's beneath them, staying at home. But we're the ones who had the real control, the influence in the home. The chores are simple, it's the shaping the children that's hard. But the little angels are a gift from heaven and it's a mother's job to raise them right. I don't get where the hardship is. What kind of a life is drinking coffee for five hours each day while some illegal immigrant raises your kids?" Sadness fell across her face. "My own daughter is missing out on the joy of raising these beautiful babies – but I'll burn in hell before I let some stranger raise them. If she has to play Bunko, fine, but these kids are coming with me. She wants to go to the mall, they're coming with me."

I nodded in agreement with her. "Where did it go wrong?"

"I've said too much already. I'm a tired old woman who misses her husband. He's been with the Lord for four years, feels more like forty. That's another thing these girls are missing out on – a life long love. Sure it takes work, but to have a person trust you for fifty years, love you your whole adult life, there wasn't a thing I wouldn't do for him. Same went for Elvin. I wish it were me that went first. When you've had what I had, it's hard to go back to being alone." She smiled, her eyes glistening.

"How do I keep them from getting my wife?" I blurted.

"Aww, don't read too much into what I've said," she wiped her eyes and turned back to her grand children.

"No, I've seen it. I know there's something going on. The women in my neighborhood, they've banded together."

"Shhhhh," the old woman "shushed" me as the young mom with the baby jogger circled past. "My daughter won't let me see the grand babies if –"

"Please. I love my wife and my kids. You have to help me. How'd you know my wife was at Bunko?"

"It's Thursday isn't it?"

"Yeah?"

"Every Thursday the local chapters have a meeting. Bunko. Sometimes they'll have a meeting on Monday, if there is special business."

"Monday? Once a month they have a PTA meeting. That's on Monday. Look, I know about the Point System, my wife already has cut me off, tell me what I should do."

Grams shook her head, "All you can do is love her, son. Maybe you'll touch her heart, bring her back. Doesn't happen much anymore, but maybe you can do it." She walked off toward the swing set.

I stood there, my blood running cold. What now? I fear that my worst nightmares are true. This housewife mafia was taking my Alicia into their fold. What did the old woman mean by "local chapters?" Did she mean that other neighborhoods, other cities in other states were also organized? Was this whole thing bigger than my little affluent neighborhood in Portland, Oregon? Did she mean that this conspiracy stretched out across the country? Around the world, even? Oh, shit.

August 18, 2003

I offered to run to the grocery store this morning. I don't know if Alicia is intentionally sand bagging or not, but there is nothing to eat in the damn house and I'm getting tired of take out. Yeah, I'm a millionaire, but getting every meal from the deli at the gourmet grocery is bleeding me dry.

I hop into the car and pick up my cell phone. I have to talk to Larry, but fearing that I may be bugged, I drive to the airport and buy a cheap ticket to Seattle and go through the metal detectors and crack aviation security to be sure I'm clean. I walk through without a problem, but to be safe I toss my cell phone in the trash.

I call Larry from a pay phone at the airport and ask him to meet me at the only safe place I can think of – Stars Cabaret.

Larry is already there when I arrive. He sits in the dark, chatting up a tall skinny red head in a satin bikini. I watch as she lets Larry give her silicone boobs a squeeze. The "too tan" doorman stamps my hand and reminds me of the two drink minimum.

"Hey Bud," I slide into the booth next to him.

"Ginger has the same boobs I bought for Kristen. She went to the same guy and everything," he laughs, impressed by what a small world it is, smaller than either of us ever thought.

I check Ginger out as she tries to talk some suit in the next booth into a table dance. "Yeah, those are exactly like Kristen's."

Larry nods then stops and turns to me, "How the hell would you know?"

"The pool dude. She's got those maracas shaking poolside practically everyday."

"Yeah, but how can you see them in that old one piece suit of hers?"

"One piece? Dude, she wears the smallest damn bikini I've ever seen. She shows off more than this girl does." Harsh, I know, but it's time to wake up and smell the coffee, Larry.

"Seriously?" he seemed genuinely perplexed, "Dammit."

"Dude, can't you tell by Kristen's tan lines? She's practically naked all day."

Larry looked deep into his ten dollar Pepsi. His tortured expression said it all.

"Cut off, huh?"

"Yep," he said. "I've never actually seen her new boobs."

"What? She got them, like six months ago."

"Eight months and eleven days, bro. At first they were 'too sensitive.' Then she got pissed because I wanted to get all over them – I mean, duh. But she was saying stuff like, 'you only want me for my new boobs.' I've never even touched them Mike. I tried to cop a feel while she was sleeping and she slapped my hand – while she was still sleeping. Five thousand points right there. Then she banned me from the bed. 'If I can't respect her as a woman, then I forfeit my right to share her bed.' What the hell, man? I'm dying here. I've got that hot American Pie walking around my house and she won't cut me off a slice." It pained me to see my buddy in such torment.

"Yep, you're cut off bud."

"And now I'm like, eighty thousand points in the hole since Doctor Robert's wife squealed on us."

A hot blonde in a star spangled bikini approaches the table, "Hi Larry."

"A little later, alright Sparkles?"

"Okay sweetie," she moved on to the next target.

"I think our phones are tapped," I said.

"What?"

"I've been sticking my nose where it doesn't belong and now they're listening in. This is probably the only cone of silence in town."

A petite brunette in black lingerie saunters up to the table, "Hi Larry," she purrs.

"Hi Trixi. I promise I'll give you a dance after my buddy and I are through talking," he smiled.

"I'm gonna hold you to that, sugar."

I stared at him, "Why does everyone know you by name?"

"Fuck you, I've been cut off for a while now dude. What do you want me to do?" he shrugged.

"Stand up for yourself. It's a little passive aggressive to tolerate being cut off and then spend all your time hanging out here in the dark."

"This from the guy who jerks off to the Howard Stern Show?"

"Where did you...man, those yentas have big mouths. Alright, fair enough. Bottom line, we're getting worked here and we have to go on the offensive."

"Yeah, and do what?"

"Well, we have to organize, for one thing. The housewives have been working together for years. They have a strategy, they're unified, they probably have by-laws and procedures and shit."

"What are you talking about?" he winced skeptically.

"Conspiracy. Our wives have enslaved us without our knowledge."

"Conspiracy? Kristen and I are going through a rough patch, that's all."

"A rough patch? Why? Brought on by whom?" I pressed.

"I guess because I bought her new boobs."

"Boobs that she begged for," I reminded.

"Yeah, until she got them and then they were my idea because I'm some kind of pervert who didn't love her the way she was."

"See that's exactly what I'm talking about. You're out eight grand, she gets what she wants and now you're eighty thousand points in the hole – eighty thousand arbitrarily assigned points that only mean anything if we accept this abuse." I stood tall on my soapbox.

A skinny, overly tan honey with huge plastic tits comes up to the table, "Hey big man. How are you doing Larry?

"Hanging in."

She brushes her hand across his crotch, "You sure are hanging."

"I'll catch you in a few alright, Porsche?"

"Sure baby."

Larry shrugs at me, "It's been a tough stretch man."

"Seriously, how often do you come in here?"

"Pretty much every day."

"Men shouldn't be forced to seek refuge in strip joints, Larry. We have to stand up for ourselves. We have to push back. This housewife mafia is brainwashing Alicia and Kristen. You're going to lose Kristen, completely, for good, if you just sit back."

"I don't know man."

"We can't do this alone, I know that. But if we both make a commitment, if we attack with a unified strategy, we can make them understand that we love them, but we're not going to play the patsy anymore. We'll need to rally a bunch of the guys. I've been thinking, if we can get all the guys at the club and you get a bunch of guys from your work, we'll have the makings of a resistance. Don't you want things the way they used to be?"

Larry didn't answer, he was hypnotized by a tall, smooth, platinum blonde in a spandex dress that was approaching from the East. She introduced herself as Silkience. Seriously, Silkience? Wasn't that a shampoo or hair conditioner or something? They're not even trying with these stripper names anymore.

"Larry, you're here early today," she seemed happy to see him.

"Yeah, quick lunch," he mumbled, staring into her eyes.

"Time for a dance with me handsome?"

Larry hesitated, looked at me and then slid out of the booth, "Sure baby. See ya later man."

She took his hand and led him to an empty booth in the back. Maybe Larry was gone. Maybe Kristen had burnt his soul to a crisp. If you're so far gone that you don't want to fight for your wife then they've already beaten you. Larry thinks he can escape his imprisonment, but if he bails on the marriage he's still going to be working for Kristen for the rest of his days.

Watching Silkience bump and grind her tight ass all over Larry brought me a level of understanding about his deal. The hours Larry spent in the dark weren't really a sexual thing. I mean, yeah, it was kind of sexual, we are talking about hot naked chicks, but really it was about being appreciated. Think about it. Larry busts his hump sixty hours a week for his wife and she acts like he's only doing what's expected. All he wants is to walk in the door after a brutal day at the office and have Kristen shake his hand like the proud General that he is and congratulate him on a job well done.

Silkience here is doing nude Pilates for a twenty spot and if she's any more appreciative the vice squad is going to bust in.

She kisses him on the cheek, looks him in the eye and says "Thanks, sweetie, want to do another?" Hell, Larry gets a warmer, more heartfelt greeting from naked chicks with goofy stage names than he gets from his own wife. How did things get this far down the road for him? I don't know. I suppose there is something reassuring about watching hot young things undress to old Guns 'N Roses played at ear bleeding levels. This naked anesthetic is more appealing that a confrontation with his wife. But chilling

173

out with the naked babes is only another way of getting hammered and, eventually, he's gonna wake up with a hangover. (On a side note, I demand a strip joint moratorium on the songs "Paradise City" and "Welcome to the Jungle." If the dancer was in grade school when these songs were released in 1987 then she is forbidden from gyrating to them. And if one more dancer says she "loves the oldies" while making reference to any Oasis, Nirvana or Green Day song, I'm going to call my Senator and have this place boarded up.)

Larry had made it clear – he wasn't going to stand with me. The "cut off" had worked to perfection. Kristen had left him in the wilderness so long his brain short-circuited. Left with nothing, Larry makes do filling the void with three minute bursts of titillation and gratitude from a perfumed stranger. It is intoxicating, I'll admit it, the smile they give you when you toss a wadded single onto the stage, the way the girls react to a simple compliment like, "You're in killer shape," – they feel appreciated and you feel appreciated. They need what Larry's giving them as much as Larry needs what they're giving him.

I have to admit that I'm relieved that Sandi/Amaretto isn't working. With the state I'm in I could easily drop a thousand dollars on Texas Couch Dances like Larry did. Hey, I'm married not dead.

August 19, 2003

I survived the interrogation after returning home after a five hour trip "to the grocery store." I walked in with two bags of groceries and a sorry story about losing my cell phone.

"What's that?" Alicia asked, referring to the day-glo stamp on the back of my hand. Damn. Fumble.

"What's what?" I tried to play stupid. Hey, it worked for Clinton, for a while anyway.

"You went to a nightclub?" Alicia starts sniffing me like a police dog.

"A nightclub? What kind of club is open at ten in the morning?" I puffed.

"That Stars Cabaret where your little caddy friend works opens at ten in the morning," she said.

Fucking hell, how did she know that? I guess I walked into that one didn't I? Damn she's good. I have to admit this is getting old, being out played and out smarted every single day. Why didn't I wash that hand stamp off? Did I think she wouldn't notice? No, I fumbled away the kick-off on this one, now my defense will have to bail me out and hold her to a field goal.

"Are you having me followed?"

"Please."

"Come on, Alicia. Like I wasn't topic number one at the Bunko meeting. 'Why is Mike poking around so much?' 'You better get him a job Alicia, he's got too much time on his hands.' 'If cutting him off from sex isn't working, then we'll shut him down for you Alicia.'"

Her jaw dropped open. Lucky shot, thank God.

"That's ridiculous."

"Is it? Alicia, let's stop this now."

"Stop what?" she asked.

"This whole charade. You hiding behind the Coalition of Angry Housewives or whatever they're calling themselves this week."

"You're talking crazy," she studied me for a moment.

I put it all on the table. "Hey, I'm not letting this deal go down. I don't know what your friends are telling you, but we both have a good thing going here. We love each other right?" She didn't say anything. Was I getting through? "What are they telling you?"

She shook her head, "Maybe you do need a job. Your imagination has gone into hyper drive," she said. A coughing, choking sound slithered up from her throat.

"What are they telling you? Are they saying you don't need me? Are they saying 'he sold his company, now just divorce that bum and live happily ever after'? Are they? It's a lie. You need me. Who is going to fix the screen door when it slams too loud? Who is going to unclog the garbage disposal when you jam it full of potato peelings? Who is going to back you up when the nanny is disciplining the children?"

"I'm not having this conversation." She started to put the groceries away. "You're not going to bait me into this."

"Then tell me what they're saying, these supposed 'friends' of yours."

She closed the fridge and turned to me, "They're saying the same thing I'm saying – you're having a mid-life crisis."

"Uh-wha-huh?" I gaped.

She was practically shaking now, "A mid-life crisis, Mike. An honest to God, text book, clinical mid-life crisis."

"Don't try and spin this thing around and make it about me. That's total bullshit. A mid-life crisis?" I laughed. "Where does that come from?"

"You bought a car for a hundred thousand dollars –"

"So what? I also bought you this house, does that sound like a man having a mid-life crisis?" I countered.

"You're masturbating to Howard Stern's television show and then bragging about it to my friends."

"That couldn't be helped," I said.

"You're out cavorting with strippers."

"I did not cavort. No cavorting occurred. And I already told you I didn't know there were going to be nude caddies at that thing. Doctor Robert punked me, I'm not wearing that one."

"What about going back to the strip joint to see Mocha?" Like she didn't remember her name, now she was just being bitchy.

"It's Amaretto and I didn't go to see her. Look, I'm sorry about that. I needed to talk with Larry and, since his phone is bugged or mine is bugged, it was the only place I knew we'd have privacy."

"And who bugged Larry's phone?"

"Why are you asking me? I should be asking you. Do you know who bugged Larry's phone?"

She just stared.

"Okay, this isn't about who bugged whose phone, the point is, I want things the way they were," I said. "You know I'd do anything for you. If you didn't know that or forgot it or some evil housewife told you it wasn't true, then hear me now, I love you. I will always love you and I don't want to play these games anymore."

"Mike, how can things be 'the way they were' with you running around thinking you're being followed?"

"Followed? Who said anything about me being followed?" A-ha.

"You did Mike."

"Okay, I get it. I'm the crazy one having the mid-life crisis. How can I be a paranoid nutzo if you are actually bugging the phones and having me followed? Are you tapping into my e-mail too? Am I leaving anything out? Am I?" She looked at me like I was hysterical, but frankly I feel like I showed great restraint.

Alicia shook her head and went back to putting away the groceries.

I slammed my hand down on the counter. "Look me in the eye and tell me I'm wrong. Tell me I'm wrong and I'll shut up and have my mid-life crisis in peace."

She turned back from the refrigerator, looked me square in the eye and said, "Mike, you're wrong."

Damn, she's a cold-blooded liar. That is scary.

August 20, 2003

Here are the cold hard facts: there is a conspiracy, housewives are taking over the world and deceptively using men as their pawns. Throughout history various attempts at world domination have been thwarted because those doing the conquering made their intentions plain. Genghis Khan, The Ottoman Turks, Napoleon and Hitler were all as subtle as a Mack truck smashing through the front window at Tiffany's. At least the Bolsheviks busted out the propaganda to help control the people. Of course, sending the occasional relative to Siberia helped underscore their point, I suppose.

These subversive housewives seemed to understand the whole "Hearts and Minds" element of war and conquest. Sure, the Suffragette movement started things off with a bang – but they took a page from The Art of War there, don't pick a fight that you can't win. These uppity chicks knew their time had finally come and everybody was sick of them whining about not being able to vote. Okay, fair enough so far. Of course, they've probably figured out by now that the democratic vote is a sham anyhow. I haven't voted in the last six elections, I prefer to make generous contributions to my favorite candidate. Have you ever tried calling your state Senator on the phone to discuss an issue? Have they taken your call? I didn't think so. Try donating a hundred grand to their re-election fund – they'll take your call then. Don't have a hundred grand to donate? Then democracy probably isn't out there working for your interests.

Next, women got a taste of the industrial revolution by working the factories during the World Wars. I read a book about "Rosie the Riveter" and gotta say I was pretty impressed. Those chicks were busting their humps as hard as any Union Joe ever has, probably harder. Wasn't like they were killing Krauts in the trenches, but without those plucky babes we might've lost the war. I think the men appreciated their efforts and I know the women were proud of what they'd accomplished.

Boys came home from overseas, married all the babes, moved to the suburbs and things were pretty much "Ozzie and Harriet" until the sixties – the decade where everybody snapped. All those mangy British rock stars came Stateside and all the girls lost their fucking minds. Maybe when they saw Mick Jagger, the Fab Four or Peter Noone from Herman's Hermits, strutting across the stage, they realized these cats were cooler than what they had waiting for them at home. Maybe a few of the jerk off men were not treating their wives sweetly, like they should've been. Who knows? I was two years old and, yes, I'm talking out of my ass here. But here's something interesting: all these women's magazines started up, throwing all kinds of smack around, bashing men and the next thing you know bras are in flames and babes are picketing for independence or equal rights or hell, maybe they liked picketing, I'm not really sure.

I think those chick magazines were designed as propaganda tools to organize the Women's Movement. Have you ever read one of these rags? And I don't mean just flipping through the glossy perfume ads trying to find a bare nipple. Read one, you'll be amazed. Because the content of Ms., Cosmopolitan and Vogue only appealed to women so it was safe to overtly display their manifestos and what not. These magazines helped unify the women, mobilize them and soon they left the kitchen and scaled the walls of the business world. Again, personally, I say do what you what to do. If some ambitious lady can come into my office and kick my ass then she deserves my job. I'll be the first to bow before my new leader.

But a funny thing happened to these female Captains of Industry on their way to world domination, something they hadn't counted on – going to work everyday sucks monkey dick. Sixty hour work weeks? Corporate politics? Office back stabbing? Welcome to the picnic, ladies. Bringing home the bacon is serious business. Did they think we were playing golf and smoking cigars all day? Okay, we do that, a lot sometimes, but we call them "client bonding sessions" or "high level meetings." Men communicate better over activities than we do over cups of coffee – but hey, we're not on trial here, back the fuck off.

So what happened next? The women looked for a loop hole, a back door out, without backtracking. In an effort to save face and still cash in, some clever, corporate women invented the Sexual Discrimination Lawsuit. "We can't hack it in the work place, but it's not our fault, men are pigs – it's their fault." Now, listen, some men are pigs. I know a few personally. Okay, I know a lot. I know some of them promised their secretaries and subordinates a raise while they had them bent over a desk. Sometimes I'm not proud of my gender, but I am saying those kind of blatant, black and white incidents were not the norm. If every sexual harassment lawsuit in the eighties stemmed from a CEO banging a female employee, you wouldn't have been able to step into a boardroom or office without stepping on someone's underwear. Didn't happen that way, those lawsuits were coming from everywhere, man. The climate of political correctness turned everything into inappropriate behavior.

A TYPICAL SCENE FROM THE WORKPLACE
CIRCA 1983:

"Hi Cheryl, what did you do this weekend?" asked Tom.

"I saw 'Flashdance,' it was awesome" replied Cheryl.

"Is that the 'dancer' movie?"

"Yeah, there is this really funny bit where Jennifer Beals takes off her bra while she's sitting in a restaurant," laughs Cheryl.

"Really? She just takes off her shirt in a restaurant?" inquired Tom, incredulously.

"No, she pulls the bra out of her shirt while keeping the shirt on."

"How do you do that? Can you do that?" Tom gaped.

Three months later, that's a lawsuit. "Tom asked me if I could take my bra off without removing my shirt," Cheryl told her lawyer.

Or, let's say Cheryl told a Blonde joke and Tom laughed – she'd cash out with three years salary and he'd be lucky to find a job selling shoes.

True story, I know this one dude who had a cute young girl in his office come up to him and say, "I had a dream about you last night. I was naked. You were naked and now, let's just say I know that you're good in bed." If that isn't sexual harassment I don't know what is. So did my buddy collect a fat settlement? No. Did this girl get the boot? No. She got a lawyer and said that my buddy was "staring at her in a sexual way while she was trying to work and it made her feel uncomfortable." If she didn't want to be checked out, maybe she shouldn't have told him she's having "naked dreams" about him. Complete bullshit. Those were dark days my friend.

Eventually, these women sucked this well dry and it was time for a new tact, the Stay At Home Wife strategy. The architects behind this movement soon discovered that if they married successful men they could achieve the wealth, status and power of a CEO without having to put in the CEO hours and deal with CEO pressure. Now a few, noble, hardworking women have ascended to these heights on the strength of their intelligence and perseverance – I'm not talking about them, I'm talking about those rabble rousers, I'm talking about the gravy trainers who are responsible for the housewife conspiracy that is subverting my wife. The math is simple, really, find a man, seduce him and he'll happily and ignorantly be your work-horse for life. Treat him right, feed him the occasional carrot and he'll plow your field until you're old. But was that good enough for these women? No, they don't want to hold up their end of the bargain – the chores, the raising of the children. We come home and the kids are sleepy faced from napping all day – they'll be up until midnight so they'll sleep all day for the housewives. The house is trashed, the laundry is still in the hamper and the cupboards are empty. Is a trip to the market really too much to ask?

But what do men do? We cave in. We say, "here's a housekeeper, here's a nanny, here's a club membership, what else do you need?" But that's still not enough, so they withhold sex, affection and appreciation and drive us to the brink of insanity and when the men become a pain in the ass, they cry "divorce." Maybe I'm reaching here, but how else do you explain a sixty percent divorce rate? The women get the money, they have no responsibility for their husband and the kids are programmed to think daddy is a monster. Ask Jack Welch, ex-CEO of General Electric or Summer Redstone, big cheese at Viacom – their wives just settled for something like a billion dollars each. A billion dollar divorce settlement? Let's do the math; that averages out to something like $147,000 per blueberry muffin, $262,000 per diaper changed and $413,000 per load of laundry. Oh, wait, Lupita the housekeeper did all that stuff for these pampered wives. My head is gonna explode.

You'd think these women would figure out a way to breed men out of existence – but no, then who would bust their asses at work for them while they're kicking it poolside? Who would unclog the toilets and clean out the gutters?

Through the years these house fraus have dissected our weaknesses, pooled their knowledge and created some kind of "invasion plan" straight out of "Invasion of the Body Snatchers." We fall in love with a beautiful woman, make a home together, start a family together and then the pod under the bed cracks open and that hottie you're sleeping with is no longer your wife. Men have been conquered without a single shot being fired. These women have been paying attention. They've watched men try to conquer each other by sending men with guns into the streets. That most often ends in death and failure. The invading army is repelled or eventually driven out by guerilla warfare. In this case the women have inserted their militia inside each one of our homes – add in a few kids and it's like they're playing a "box and one" defense on every single man in the country. Most of the men don't even know they've been conquered or they figured it out too late to do anything about it.

If you're reading this, you may think this journal is the hysterical ravings of a madman, a man so sex starved he can't think straight. But I ask you to consider the evidence. I submit the following as proof of a conspiracy. Answer "yes" or "no" to the following questions:

TAKE THE "IS YOUR WIFE PART OF THE STAY AT HOME WIVES CONSPIRACY?" TEST:

1. Does your wife think she can read your mind?
2. When your wife rambles on about family stuff or soap operas, do you hear "blah-blah-blah Victor and Nikki blah-blah-blah"?
3. In sustained conversations with your wife do you suffer from headaches, dizziness or shortness of breath?
4. Has your wife declared your college buddies "off limits" because they're a "bad influence" on you?
5. Does your wife think you "chew your food too loudly?"

6. Does your wife try to make a link between the new dent on the fender she forgot to tell you about and the amount of sports you watch on television?

7. Does your wife ignore your rational explanations for coming home late from work?

8. Does she blame you for feeling "self conscious" at parties?

9. Does your wife hold you responsible for her weight gain?

10. Does your wife have time to go through your pockets but can't find time to take your "good shirts" to the cleaners?

11. Does your wife claim her job is harder than your job?

12. Have you ever been locked out of the bedroom "for no good reason?"

13. Does your wife regularly attend a neighborhood Bunko game?

14. Does your wife regularly attend an Oprah Book Club meeting?

15. Has your wife ever attended a Creative Memories scrap booking seminar?

16. Has your wife had Botox injections and then denied it?

17. Does your wife spend more than five hours a week at Starbucks?

18. Has your wife ever made disparaging comments about any of the following: Don Imus, Jim Rome, Rush Limbaugh or Howard Stern?

19. Has your wife ever fondly quoted any of the following: Kathy Lee Gifford, Oprah Winfrey, Rosie O'Donnell or Dr. Phil?

20. Does your wife refer to your children as "your kids" only when they're in trouble?

16-20 "yes" answers = "She's Got You By the
   Short and Curlies"
11-15 "yes" answers = "There May Still Be Hope For You"
6-10 "yes" answers = "You're an Unobservant Prick"
0-5 "yes" answers = "Complete and Total Denial"

For the record, I answered "yes" to all twenty questions, so don't feel too bad. These are the cold, hard facts as I've come to realize them. I was in the dark for so long, maybe you have been too. Even with this new understanding, I'm not giving up or giving in. Somehow I'm going to get to the root of this housewife mafia – find the Godfather, so to speak, find this monster and decapitate her. That's my only hope, our only hope.

August 21, 2003

Oh my God! She did it. She finally went and did it. She threw out my couch. Alicia fucking gave away the Beast.

I'd gone cruising to Starbucks, hoping that the punk barista would magically reappear – she didn't. Think I was followed by a woman driving a Denali, but not sure, because there were eleven of those tanks on the road. Anyway, I bounce into the house with a pound of Breakfast Blend and Alicia says "Thanks, hon," like it's just a normal day.

Then I walk into my den to watch the Mariners continue their slow fade from playoff contention and what don't I see? My FUCKING couch! That couch was my sanctuary, my bed away from bed, my monument to a once proud and powerful sex drive. It was also the keeper of a very valuable beer stain collection (I had actually identified and labeled stains from 57 different beers including rare and discontinued brands like Rainier, Buckhorn, Schmidt, original Miller, Pabst Blue Ribbon and Henry's). That couch was the last physical shred of my identity – the Beast was a part of me.

"Alicia?" I bellowed.

She casually stepped into the doorway, "Yeah, Mike?"

"Yeah, Mike? Yeah, Mike?" My face contorted until it cramped up, "The Beast? Where's the Beast?"

She looked confused, "The Beast?"

"My fucking couch, Alicia," I shrieked like a monkey with his nuts caught in a hornet's nest.

Alicia sighed with relief, "Oh, the couch. I was wondering, 'he's cranky today'…the couch, yeah, I gave it away."

I must've heard her wrong. "You gave it away?"

"Yep."

"I gave it away."

"You gave it away?"

"Are you okay?"

"My couch. The couch I got in college from Arvid Straum?"

"The old, smelly couch, yeah," her relaxed demeanor mocked me.

"Get it back."

"I can't."

"Who'd you give it to? I'll go get it back."

"You can't get it back. I donated it to those people who collect for the underprivileged," she said.

"Which people? The "underprivileged thing" is going around these days. Was it the United Way?"

She craned her neck, perplexed, "I don't think so."

"The Goodwill?"

She carefully squinted and cocked her head as if she was going to read the answer off the ceiling.

Meanwhile, my teeth were about to snap off, "The Salvation Army? The Arc? The Union Gospel Mission?"

Her face brightened, "Maybe it was a church group."

She was jacking me up like a pro.

"Don't do me like this," I begged.

Breaking character, she threw her arms up, "Come on Mike, that couch was old and it reeked. One of the guys loading it onto the truck literally gagged."

"That couch was mine. It was mine, it wasn't yours to give away. I've had that couch at every place I've lived since Ivy Hall...that couch is a part of me. You knew that Alicia. You knew that."

"If I'd known it was going to be a big hairy deal I would've left the dumb old couch here until it rotted away, which, by the way, would probably have been another two weeks. Okay, I'm sorry. Are you seriously going to make a thing over the couch?"

"Yeah, I am, Alicia. That is total bullshit. We both know what's going on here."

"Oh, goodie, more about your conspiracy theory? Alright, I confess, my friends hired an Al-Qaeda sleeper cell to kidnap your couch and I'm covering up for them."

"Mock me if you want. But I want you to know that I know. Okay? I know. The jig is up. One day soon I'm gonna turn on the lights and watch the rats scatter for cover. Okay? Tell your Bunko team that I'm coming for them. This marriage is between you and me. They've got nothing to do with us."

I walked over to a pitcher of flowers and shouted into them, "Did you catch that ladies? Game over."

"Mike, what are you doing?"

"The whole house is bugged, right? That way you don't have to waste time repeating everything at your clan meetings."

"Mike, this is embarrassing," she said.

"Embarrassing? Embarrassing because YOU'VE LOST CONTROL OF YOUR MAN?" I shouted into a lamp. "Hah! That's it isn't it? Embarrassing because I'm not going along with the program anymore? Because I can see the world for what it is? Guess what, pretty soon all my buddies will be with me. Men everywhere will know the truth. What do you think of that?" I screamed into the microwave oven.

Alicia stepped back, "You're not having a mid-life crisis, you're having a nervous breakdown."

"Oh sure, I see the second gunman lurking on the grassy knoll and I'm the crazy one, eh? I see Elvis shopping for fresh fruit and I'm nutzo? I see the Wizard behind the curtain and guess what? He's a chick, baby," I yelled up at the microphone hidden in the track lighting. "Are you getting all this? A hard rain's gonna fall ladies. The Point System? It's over. From now on a husband and wife will give unto each other because they love each other, not because of a stupid ass scorecard you keep on a secret ledger. Cut us off from sex? I don't think so. We don't like that one. Why do you think we're so fucking uptight all the time? Let me explain how it's gonna be. The man is King of his castle, right? And the Queen, she hangs out all day with her servants trying on jewelry and planning costume balls and what not. Now if the King, after a long day of negotiating a treaty or jousting with his knights or some such shit, needs some lovin,' well guess what? The Queen is duty bound to give it up. Let me tell you friends, there is going to be some banging in this peaceable little kingdom tonight. If the castle is rocking, don't come a knocking," my voice echoed up the chimney.

"Are you finished?" she said.

"Where's my damn couch?"

"Gone forever," she spun around and left the room.

August 22, 2003

I'm a little groggy, didn't sleep very well last night. I was pissed about losing my couch, but it's possible that I over played my hand with Alicia. Never was any good at poker. My favorite part of the game was gloating and taunting – before the cards were laid down. In business, war, and apparently, love it's considered a tactical error to let your opponent know exactly what you know.

Alicia took some responsibility for the couch incident by leaving the bedroom door unlocked. She knew I had no place else to sleep. Alicia the Merciful, right? Throw out my couch and then expect me to say, "thanks honey" when I crawl into the bed?

But my slumber was short lived, interrupted by a sharp pain in my lower back. I had suffered through the passing of kidney stones years before – like I needed that right now, because let me tell you, passing kidney stones is like giving birth to razor blades.

"Honey?" Alicia whispered.

"Uh, yeah."

"You're snoring."

"Huh?"

"You're snoring. Roll over."

"I'm snoring?"

"Roll over, okay, baby?"

"I'm not snoring."

"Just roll over baby."

"Huh? Uh, okay," I grunted.

I turned onto my side and the pain in my back subsided – her knee returned to her side of the bed. At least it wasn't kidney stones. I quickly descended back into the comforting darkness of sleep.

A couple hours later, or maybe it was only ten minutes later, the shooting pain returned. Through the veil of sleep I heard her silky voice.

"Mike?"

"Huh?"

"You're doing it again."

"Uh, what?"

"Snoring."

"What? I'm snoring?"

"Yeah. Roll over onto your stomach."

"Huh?"

"Roll over. You're snoring," she said.

"I'm not snoring."

"Mike, just roll over."

"Huh? Uh, okay," I grunted.

I rolled onto my stomach. My neck twisted at an impossible angle. Again I tried to jump start my slumber. I burrowed in, closed my eyes, exhaled deeply a few times – but it didn't take, I snuck a glance at the digital clock on the dresser, it read "2:47 a.m."

As I watched the clock roll over to "3:13 a.m.," the room began to shake. Alicia was squeezing my shoulder, rocking me back and forth.

"Mike?"

"Huh?"

"You're snoring again," she whispered.

Snoring? Baby, I ain't even sleeping.

"Uh, what?" I mumbled.

"Maybe you should roll onto your back?" she suggested sweetly.

Back to where we started, eh? There aren't any more sides to roll onto, so what choice do we have?

"Why?"

"You're snoring again."

"I, uh, I am?"

"Just roll over, okay Mike?"

"Huh? Uh, okay."

Like a whale on a sandbar, I flopped onto my back. Alicia kissed me on the cheek and she promptly fell asleep. As I lay there, staring at the ceiling, watching night surrender to morning, I remembered a story I'd heard about the concentration camps of World War II. In an effort to destroy the spirits of their prisoners, the Nazis would awaken their prisoners in the middle of the night and force them outside in the cold for a roll call. The prisoners would stumble back to their bunks, try to sleep and then, shortly thereafter, the whistles would blow again. Again, the prisoners would be rousted and forced out into the cold. Over and over until dawn the sleep deprived prisoners would be awakened and called outside. Fucking Nazis and their psychological torture – it all felt very real to me right about now. Snoring? My flatulent ass. I suspect the Stay at Home Wives have been watching the History Channel.

August 23, 2003

A mercifully quiet day, Alicia took the kids to the pool and I've been packing for our trip back east over the Labor Day weekend, a family reunion with my crew. Gonna be tough to put on a good front for the relatives with the walls coming down around here, but I'm determined to soldier on, those Stay at Home Wives aren't going to break me.

Dragged a love seat into my den to watch the Mariners game. Didn't compare to my old couch, but I was so buzzed from lack of sleep I wasn't going to let it harsh me out. I flipped on the TV, one hundred and ninety one channels of snow – I did let that harsh me out.

I peeked out of my bedroom window on the second floor – no satellite dish? What the fuck?

I searched the grounds and finally found the dish, what was left of it anyway. It was down by the aborted vegetable garden/bark pile. There it lay, smashed to bits with a suspicious looking tire print on it. I matched the tire print up with a tire on the riding lawn mower and, voila – it didn't take Columbo to deduce what had happened here. Obviously, the wind blew the satellite dish onto the lawn where Carlos accidentally ran over it with the riding mower. All very logical, completely understandable, nothing wrong with this picture at all... what am I, a fucking moron? You think you can play me that easy? Accident my ass. This is a clear and blatant act of sabotage. Something this heinous and cruel shatters the Geneva Convention. The United Nations is going to hear about this. You just don't mess with a man's satellite television, especially on game day. Cold shit, Maynard, cold shit.

August 24, 2003

Another tough night of "snoring." Finally, right about the time my eyes started to bleed from lack of sleep, I retreated to the garage, stretched out in the remarkably roomy Mercedes SUV and settled into a solid sleep zone. The seatbelt buckle dug into my spleen, but I pretended it was Alicia's knee so I felt right at home.

Around 3:30 a.m. I heard tapping on the windshield.

"Sorry Officer, I thought I could park here overnight," I blurted out. Alicia opened the door.

"What are you doing Mike?"

"Uh, what?"

"I wondered where you went. I looked all over the house."

"Oh, yeah, we'll I'm here."

"Couldn't you sleep?

"Huh?"

"Couldn't you sleep?" she repeated.

"Not with you waking me up every half hour to tell me I'm snoring."

"I was thinking we should have that checked out. There's an operation you can get, Debra's husband just had it. He sleeps like a baby now," she said.

"You woke me up to tell me that?"

"Sorry."

"You fucking saw me sleeping just now, right?"

"I thought you'd be more comfortable in bed," she said.

"But you saw me sleeping."

She just stood there, waiting, waiting for what?

"I'm fine here," I said finally.

"Okay, Mr. Grump Grump, see you in the morning."

Nice. She kept me talking just long enough to totally wake me up.

What am I doing sleeping in the car? I can't pretend that I'm winning this war.

August 25, 2003

Alicia is bringing the house. Linebackers, safeties, corners, even the D-line is stunting. Even if I see the blitz coming, I can't seem to audible out of the play in time to avoid getting killed. The receivers don't run their hot routes, I can't throw the ball away quickly enough and she blindsides me again. Okay, enough with the sports analogy, here's what happened today.

I'm holding six tickets to the Mariners but I've just been informed that we're not going. Why you ask? Because Cassie has to watch the neighbor's dog while they're in Mexico.

"We've had these tickets for two months. They're playing the Angels, I've already paid for the suite at the Elliot Bay Hyatt Regency," I protested.

"I'm sorry Mike, Cassie can't just leave the dog."

"Why not? It's a dog. Put him in the garage, give him a bowl of food and a bowl of water and we'll see him tomorrow," I raised my palms to the sky.

Alicia shook her head, "What kind message would that send to Cassie about responsibility?"

She was trying to get under my skin. Mission accomplished. I was losing my mind. "What? Responsibility? You can't ditch the family once plans are made, isn't that a message we should be teaching our kids?"

"I think you're being a tad selfish. These are your plans, not Cassie's. She's four. She doesn't care if Ichiro makes a touchdown," she said.

Alicia is grinding me now. She knows sports, she had brothers, she knows there are no touchdowns in baseball –

Alicia's trying to get me to amp out.

An idea hits me, "Alright, we'll take the dog then." Hah. Return volley. Didn't see that one coming, did you?

Alicia shrugged, "Fine."

"Fine," I huffed.

I don't know what Alicia slipped that dog, but about ten minutes north of Vancouver that mutt's hairy anus exploded. That fucking dog spray painted the back of the Mercedes with the stankiest doggy diarrhea ever in the history of the world. The Pentagon would kill to get their hands on this toxic formula. Anthrax? Agent Orange? Mustard Gas? Those chemical weapons are fine perfumes compared to this evil strain of liquid dog shit. My eyes watered and I had the dry heaves all the way back to Portland.

I should have spent the afternoon on the first base line at Safeco Field watching Jamie Moyer one-hit Anaheim, instead I spent the past two hours wrestling with the Shop Vac, and the industrial strength cleaning machine barely touched the hideous doggie mess. Now the car smells like soggy, Pine Sol scented dog shit and so do I.

If I honestly assess the past few days, and the unholy beating I'm taking, I'm man enough to admit that calling out Alicia may have been, quite possibly, a huge fucking mistake. I have awakened a sleeping giant. Remember "Tora Tora Tora?" Admiral Yamamota knows how I feel.

How do I compete with her relentless pursuit of victory? The purity of her effort to shatter my soul is chilling. She didn't think twice about tossing out my sacred couch or sacrificing her virginal new Mercedes to the cause. This battle of the sexes is quickly escalating into a steel cage death match. Somebody hand me a folding chair.

August 26, 2003

Want to hear something funny? Seriously, this is really fucking funny. I got laid last night. I'm not making this up.

Out of nowhere Alicia rocked me to Pluto and back. What am I supposed to do with that? All week she's been waging a guerilla campaign against me and now this? I know, I know, "hearts and minds, hearts and minds." It's probably some kind of strategic ploy, but frankly I didn't care. She felt so good in my arms. Usually, Alicia's not what you'd call a screamer, but let's just say my ears are ringing so loud today I swear I've got a Pete Townshend grade case of Tinnitus brewing. But like Pavlov's dog, the high pitched squeal in my head is making my mouth water even now. Yes, I'm proud to say my wife practically screamed herself hoarse in my arms. We tried stuff we'd never tried – dangerous stuff, fun stuff. I admit to being scared for a few dicey seconds here and there, but if she were trying to kill me, I would've died happy.

Hey, there's a new angle for assisted suicide nobody has thought of: screwing a guy to death. An injection of a lethal poison is so impersonal, why not turn Bambi loose on Great Uncle Bob? Dude dies happy without withering away in front of his family. You know, this form of "assist-ed suicide" may not take on the first treatment. And it's possible that if he survives six or eight treatments, Great Uncle Bob's condition may actually improve. Now he has a reason to live, he has to hang on until his next "suicide session."

Today I'm living proof that sex fixes everything. I vaguely remember something about a conspiracy, but I don't fucking care. So what? Last night I was thrown around the sack like a rag doll by a hot soccer mom who knows how to use her body – which continues to defy gravity, by the way. Maybe Alicia hasn't been using sex as a weapon. Maybe she finally realized she needed it as bad as I did. She also probably realized that she needed me as much as I needed her. She had surrendered. At last she had surrendered. By standing up for myself, by standing firm in the face of neighborhood housewife conspiracy, I had made things right. From now on things are going to be the way they used to be. Man, we hadn't gone at it like that since…since, I can't remember when. I'm not sure anyone has ever had better sex, anywhere, ever, than I had last night. Life is good.

August 27, 2003

Where is the idiot who wrote that last entry? Would somebody please fucking kill him? Actually, forget it, that fucker is dead already.

How could I be so stupid? How could I let Alicia spin my head around with a simple roll in the hay? Okay, to call it a simple roll in the hay is unfair. But on the day after I can say it surely was not the best sex ever in the history of the world. Though it may have been the best sex I've ever had. It certainly cracked the top three, ranking right alongside that time on the pool table with Mrs. Bederman.

I was a senior in high school, she was running for city council and was the mother of a bud from school. I was volunteering for her campaign, putting signs in yards and handing out flyers. One day I dropped by to pick up some extra signs. She led me down to the game room and, wham-bam, next thing I know I'm rubbing the felt off the Bederman family pool table with my bare ass. She's riding me like a bronco, whooping and hollering like a cowgirl in the rodeo. I learned two important things that day: one, volunteering has it's own rewards and two, you can get an unbelievable rug burn from felt.

Number two on the all time list was with Alicia, on the roof of her parents' house one hot August night. We were house sitting for her folks a couple of months after we got engaged and for some reason decided to drag a sleeping bag onto the roof. One thing leads to another, and next thing you know, we're going at it. I'm pumping, she's grinding, I'm on top, she's on top, whatever, doesn't matter, every little thing is clicking, you know? Anyway,

203

we're rocking so hard that the sleeping bag begins to slip a little, but we don't stop – we barely even notice. We grip each other tighter and keep the beat going. We're going harder and faster, lost in our little world of sleeping bag sex – and then the sleeping bag starts to slide toward the roof line like a toboggan on a snowy hill. Alicia cries out, not from fear, she's climaxing with the vigor of a violent epileptic seizure. I almost had to stick her panties in her mouth to keep her from biting off her tongue. Then, a split second later, and about five feet from the roof line, I peak with an orgasm that proved the existence of God and he was good. For the next second or so I was at complete peace with the universe. I may have actually enjoyed an elusive, magical moment of ultimate clarity.

Then Alicia screamed again, this time out of fear, and, with what may have been a life saving reflex, I jammed my arm into the gutter to prevent us from sailing right off the roof. We stopped inches from the edge. We lay there on the cedar shakes, peeking over the edge of the roof and laughed. We remained entwined, exhausted, precariously balanced on her parents' roof for a good hour. It was awesome. Then, my arm began to tingle. I shook it to get the feeling back, which is when Alicia noticed that my elbow was on the wrong side of my arm. From the elbow down, my right arm was freaking backwards.

The emergency room doctor told me he'd never seen such a clean break. Funny, I didn't feel any pain. None. So, sex on the roof is number two. Could've been number one, but I had to wear that damn cast on my arm for six weeks.

So, what about last night? I guess last night moves all

the way up the charts to number three, with a bullet. But that was last night and this morning I feel like swallowing that bullet.

I came down to breakfast to find my kids crowded around the table gluing glitter onto MY BEATLES CDs! All of them. Cassie had taken a piece of string and connected "Rubber Soul," "Revolver," "Sgt. Pepper's Lonely Heart's Club Band" and, what's left of "The Beatles For Sale," and, I think, "Help!"

"Look Daddy, I'm making a mobile out of these little mirrors," she said.

"Mine has a smiley face," Timothy said, showing off the big adhesive grin he'd painted across "The White Album." There was a pain piercing my chest, but, yeah, Timmy was kinda cute. Then I saw that the leather bound case that once housed the Beatles entire British catalog, it lay crushed under the leg of Andy's chair.

"I gave these jay walkers glitter heads," said Andy, waving the defaced "Abbey Road" cover.

I just nodded my head in resignation, "Ringo could use a little more glitter," I said.

Brent laughed, "Andy said you'd get all mad and loud."

"Why is that?"

"He thought you wouldn't like us doing all this art."

"But I made sure to pick out old music so you would-n't be mad at us," chimed in Timothy.

"Good thinking." I refused to let this get me down. I had sex last night. I had great sex last night. "Is everybody packed?"

"What for?" Andy asked.

"We're going to New York to see Nana and Uncle Robbie and Old Uncle Fred and..." the kids exchanged a confused look. Uh-oh.

"Where's your mother?" I asked.

"Mommy's helping Grand Ma with her suitcase," Cassie said.

Grand Ma? Oh, shit.

The other shoe dropped. As it turns out, Alicia's mom is having her house flea bombed and needs a place to stay. Flea bombed? She doesn't even have pets. Meanwhile, we have a flight to New York City in three hours. We're one hour from leaving for the airport when Alicia spills it.

She speaks in that quiet, controlled voice of hers. "We're not going with you," she said.

"But, I, uh, what?"

"I can't leave my mom here alone."

"Why not? She lives alone at her house. She can live alone here."

"She'll feel like I'm abandoning her," Alicia explained.

"So abandon her. I'll kick her to the curb for you. I'll put her up at the Hotel Vintage Plaza for the weekend and she can feel abandoned in a five star hotel."

"Mike, she'll hear you," Alicia whispered.

"I can't believe this."

"It's probably all for the best."

She's doing it to me again. I felt my blood pressure shove my brain against the top of my skull. "It's all for the best? How's that exactly? I show up for a family reunion without my family, you're right, that is better. I'll do imitations of the kids for my mom – who hasn't seen them for two years, by the way."

"She's welcome here anytime. It's not my fault she never visits," Alicia snapped.

"That's not the point and you know it."

"Besides, school starts in a few days, that trip would've worn them out. They can't start a new school year all exhausted and tired," she said in a condescending tone.

"And you bring that up now?" I checked my watch, "two hours and fifty minutes before the flight?"

"I brought it up when you planned this, but you weren't listening to me."

"So this isn't you bailing on plans that have been set for eight months, this is me being a bad listener?"

She shrugged. Her expression was relaxed, almost sympathetic, as if to say "Hey, Mike, I'd help you if I could, but it's out of my control."

The real head spinner is that this is the same woman that fucked me to within an inch of my life last night. The same woman who left teeth marks on the back of my neck, right after whispering "You're going to feel a little sting." When we were making love, there was no room for interpretation. What we were trying to say to each other was made perfectly clear. The message was communicated simply, directly, without words to get in the way. If only there was some form of code where we could use physical contact to communicate. Like, I stick my tongue in her ear and she knows that I want to take her out for a nice meal. I don't know, this whole using words thing isn't working for me.

A thought crossed my mind: what if, through some kind of housewife to husband mistranslation, we were using separate vocabularies when we had a conversation? Say that a word like "cat" really means "purple" to my wife. That would explain the Catch-22 like insanity. For example, Alicia says something like "Hey, honey, let's all go to the movies." But what she actually means is something like, "Hey, honey, I'm never ever going to change the oil in the car, and when the motor finally seizes and the engine block cracks I'm going to plead ignorance and expect you to buy me a new rig." That would explain it. Every word means something different than I think it means. Yes, that's it. That makes sense. Everything I know is wrong.

August 28, 2003

My flight to NYC was delayed three hours. Surprised? I'm not.

After sitting on the plane for an hour, the captain's voice crackled over the public address, "We made some adjustments to the hydraulics, but we're not real happy with how the flaps are responding, so we're bringing in another bird. We're going to 'deplane' in a few moments so we can make room for the new plane and we will begin the 'replaning' process as soon as we can. We hope to be on our way in the next hour or so."

Bad hydraulics? My sweet ass, you and I both know the housewife mafia is behind this one. Alicia made a call to Kristen, Kristen made a call to another housewife who placed a call to the mechanic's wife and she threatened to destroy his collection of Playboy magazines. A collection he had hidden in the attic that he thought nobody knew about. The housewives are that thorough and that ruthless – bet on it.

That's all right. I'm going to be waiting and watching, looking for my opening. I'm resigned that this is my destiny. I no longer have control of my own life. I know that now. Maybe I never had it, but it seemed like I did. I was just another ignorant, blind man, but I enjoyed the illusion of making decisions and affecting change in my little world. But now I have seen behind the curtain. I can't go back to the way things were. The genie won't go back into the bottle. I guess my destiny is to be the keeper of this terrible truth. I'm going to keep writing everything I see and hear in this journal and one day soon I'll blow the lid off this whole conspiracy. Who will listen to one man? A semi-literate, rambling man at that? I don't know. But I swear to you I'm telling the truth and when men read this, they will know that I'm telling the truth. They'll start to put two and two together. And pretty soon, it won't be one man it will be a dozen. Then a dozen will become a hundred, our numbers will multiply and we'll have our own damn Equality Movement. Ain't that a hoot? It may take two years, it may take ten, but we're gonna turn the tables on the stay at home housewives.

Bottom line, this isn't about me. I'm fighting for a better America for my boys. One day when my son is grown and married and he's heading out the door to watch Monday Night Football with his buds at the local watering hole, I want him to hold his head high. When his wife stops him at the front door, he'll be able to say:

"Sweet cheeks, I'm going down to the Leaky Roof to watch football with the guys."

"When will you be home?" she'll ask.

"Uh, after the game is over," he'll say.

His pretty wife will smile, "Oh, okay."

"Oh, by the way, the Bud Girls are going to be there," he'll add. "Probably bra-less again."

"In that case, unscrew your penis and I'll put it in the safe," she'll say. After a second, they'll both laugh, because the wife is joking. She doesn't have a safe and his penis is not detachable.

"You should probably put on some lingerie because when I get home I'll be drunk and horny."

His wife will be flushed with anticipation, "Of course. Is the crotchless body stocking alright?"

"Yeah, sure, fourth time this week though. Don't you have anything else?"

"I have been saving a new outfit for a special occasion," she'll say.

"Hey, Monday Night Football babe, does it get more special than that?"

"No honey, it doesn't. I'll be waiting," she'll say.

Then they'll end up doing it right there on the entry way floor, before he goes to the game. Then, he'll enter the bar like the big swinging dick that he is and explain to the fellas why he missed the first quarter of the game.

Hey, it may not be much, but it's a dream…a dream of a brighter future for men everywhere.

On the plane to New York, I sit next to a former Portland Trailblazer. For his own protection I won't reveal his identity. I'm going to have to be more discrete in case this journal should ever fall into the wrong hands. I don't want to risk the lives of men brave enough to stand up to this conspiracy.

Anyway, this former hoop star talked to me about his days in the ABA and NBA. Touching stories of the fame and the money. Looking back, he laughs at how little he actually made considering he was one of the top performers in his trade. Compared to the NBA players of today it's ridiculous how little he made, but this guy was appreciative of the amazing life he enjoyed as a player. He traveled the country, stayed in five star hotels, met all kinds of hot women and basked in the adoration of the fans while playing a kid's game. We talked about the players of today and he isn't bitter about the huge salaries they're pulling in. He isn't pissed that his success propelled the popularity of the Association into the stratosphere. What does chap his hide are the ungrateful, multi-millionaire punk ass motherfuckers who are ruining the game. The drugs, the idiotic decisions, the contempt for the fans – the same fans who pay $100 a ticket to watch these jag-offs brick free throws.

As we talk, I start to wonder if there was a sports agent who was paying attention to the stay at home wives operation. This new NBA seemed to be based on the house wife model: more money for less work. Is there a way to have our cake and eat it too? Is there a way to grab all the money without having to do our job and disrespect everyone we cross in the process? Sound familiar to you?

And look at the emergence of the stage mom in basketball. All these high school kids getting shoved right into the NBA? Each game features 200 close-ups and 50 interviews of the women who raised these budding billionaire brats. She just sits there with a grin on her face. Saying she'd be "just as proud if her son were a sanitation engineer." Somehow, I don't think so. She saw this kid grow to be a foot taller than every other kid in his class and she did the math. She kicked the husband out of the picture, or drove him away using one of a hundred published techniques and now it's payday. She sits there with Jim Gray on her lap, smiling for the camera and collecting a big chunk of her son's paycheck. Come to think of it, I'll bet the NBA is now being run by a housewife or maybe David Stern is a hapless puppet being operated by his wife. Hey, I'm just following the evidence here. That would explain a few things. The NBA, an institution loved by men, is being driven into the ground. Does that sound like something a man would do? No. And leaving Stern out front as the fall guy? I smell another spin of the stay at home wives propaganda wheel.

August 29, 2003

I was having breakfast at the St. Regis Hotel waiting for my brother to pick me up and looking forward to a day of explaining to relatives why my family wouldn't be joining me for the family reunion. But I felt a strange sense of peace sitting here in this gorgeous, old hotel – I felt like I was in a different world. Heck, the City felt like a civilization unto itself. Now, I'm not one of those snobs who thinks NYC stretches to the Mississippi and LA is the only city out West that's using paper money. My old friend Ross used to say, "We're doing real good here in Oregon. Sure things have been tough since the bottom fell out of the beaver pelt market, but luckily I had also invested in the Spotted Owl, so I'm financially secure."

But let's face it, how can you compare the suburbs of Oregon to New York City? Classic Brownstones instead of the generic McMansions, actual city blocks instead of cul-de-sacs, Iranians driving yellow taxi cabs instead of Soccer Moms driving SUVs, and I especially love getting the morning paper from a newsstand vendor yelling "You gonna buy that? This ain't a library," instead of fishing it out of that plastic Koi pond in the front yard. Everything and everyone seemed so different, probably because I've been up to my neck in this suburban housewife conspiracy. But away from the trappings of the suburbs, I was able to think my first clear thought in days. For a minute, I felt like I'd be able to figure this whole mess out. Were things really so bad? Instead of declaring war with my neighborhood housewife mafia maybe we could draft a treaty, find a way to slow down this arms race, find a way to smooth things over with Alicia?

Watching New York bristle with its usual frenetic energy, I realized that life goes on. The housewives may have a stranglehold on my block, but the world still spins. Maybe since leaving the ranks of the working man, I've made my life too small. Maybe it was me that was encroaching on the domain of the housewife and not the other way around. Why do I care what store we shop at? Who gives a fuck? Right? Why not let Alicia do her stuff the way she wants to do it? Everything I've been worrying about is irrelevant, the housewives don't really control anything. If I didn't want to buy Alicia a Mercedes then she wouldn't have a Mercedes. When I get home I'm going to look into investment opportunities and find a new project to sink my teeth into. I need a new deal. Alicia and the house fraus may run the cul-de-sac, we'll give 'em that one, but entrepreneurs like me make America swing. As for Alicia ditching me on this trip? I'm over it. Can you blame her? Traveling across the continent with four kids, for what, a visit with my family? Hell, I wouldn't cross the street to share a pizza with her family. I'm glad we've had this talk, I'm feeling much better about things.

As I'm sitting in the restaurant, enjoying an actual, honest to God, New York cup of coffee, my peace is interrupted by these two yammering yentas at the next table. The tall, slender one is probably mid-thirties, the shorter chick with the big eyes could be forty or fourteen. I'd steal a glance and she'd look like a spunky teen, but then she'd turn her head, the light would catch her differently and she'd look forty. They're probably up from Jersey to play in the city for the weekend. Anyway, they are going on and on about the cream being a "little off" so I offer them mine just to shut them up.

"Please, take mine," I set the cream down on their table.

"We couldn't," 40/14 said.

"Thanks," said Stretch.

"Not a problem. Can't take Manhattan without cream for your coffee." We all shared one of those awkward "that wasn't funny, but what else can we do but laugh" moments. I turned back to my bagel.

"So are you from the city?"

"Used to be," I said.

"Back to visit family?" asked 40/14.

Okay, I guess it's gonna be small talk with the Outlet Mall Twins until my slacking brother finally shows up. He's probably watching me from a secure location near the lobby, right now. Bastard. But he'll pay, he'll pay.

"I am indeed. And you? What brings two lovely young women to the Big Apple?"

"A much deserved weekend away," smiled Stretch.

I was temporarily blinded when a beam of light reflected off the enormous diamond cluster on 40/14's wedding ring. "Yeah? Are your husbands sleeping in?" I ignorantly asked.

They both erupted in laughter. I mean, for real, their bodies shook with deep, satisfying laughter.

"Dumb question, huh?" I smiled.

"Well, I have three kids and she has four little ones and we told our husbands we had to get away for a girl's weekend," 40/14 said earnestly.

"Sometimes you need to get away from it all," echoed Stretch.

"Yeah, I hear ya. Give your husbands a little time behind the wheel of the mini-van." Listen to these bimbos, thinking they're going to get sympathy from me? They don't know that I know what I know.

"That's right," said 40/14.

"You must have kids."

"Four."

"How does your wife do it?" asked Stretch.

"She's a saint. Actually, I've written the Pope for a special dispensation." I smile to let them know that I was joking, I hadn't actually nominated my wife for sainthood. "You know yourself, raising four kids is like running an orphanage."

Stretch smiled. "Your wife is a regular Mother Theresa, letting you go on vacation by yourself."

"If you call a family reunion a vacation," I winked.

They both laugh. Finally, an easy room. Then a dark thought floated to the top of my brain. "Listen to how these housewives are talking. Anything ringing a bell here Mike? They're comparing a stay at home wife who hangs out at Starbucks and nags her maid with Mother Theresa, a selfless woman who devoted her life to serving the destitute in Calcutta. They're in on it Mike, I'm telling you. Find out for sure if this conspiracy has really gone national. Find out if the old woman in the park was right about the local chapters."

I pulled a chair up to their table. The two housewives were taken aback by my forward gesture, but smiled politely nevertheless.

"Actually, I earned this trip. I built up fifty thousand points with my wife and cashed them in on a weekend alone in New York," I said.

Their faces turned to stone.

Direct hit. I moved in for the kill. "I know, amazing, huh? Took me almost three years to build up fifty thousand points. And it wasn't easy, let me tell you," I nodded. "How many points are your guys earning this weekend?"

Both housewives looked at me suspiciously.

"Relax. I know all about the Point System. You're not letting anything out of the bag here," I reassured them.

40/14 finally broke the silence, "Uh, fifty, fifty points," she said. Stretch and 40/14 exchanged a nervous glance. They were engaging in a forbidden conversation.

"Wow, you're generous. Fifty, for one weekend? I'm jealous. I had to siphon out my mother-in-law's septic tank with a garden hose to earn fifty points. Your men have it easy. Here's a tip, we don't play with our kids to earn points we play with them because we love them. Give your guys 25 points and they'll be happy." I laid my best Opie Cunningham smile on them.

You should have seen these house fraus twitch. They exchanged a look, apparently trying to decide whether to bolt from the table or find out how I knew so much. "Your wife told you about the Point System?" asked 40/14.

"Oh, sure. I wasn't a big fan at first but I've come to realize that it's necessary all the same. I mean, without it there would be chaos, right? Men wanting sex all the time, never doing any chores around the house, using their job at the office as an excuse to relax and watch sports when they come home. Where would we be without the Point System?" I nodded reverently.

"You earned fifty thousand points?" asked Stretch.

"Uh-huh, but, really, my wife and I are so in synch it really wasn't that hard. It's like Dr. Phil says,

"Love is like oxygen. Get too much, you get too high, not enough and you're gonna die."

"Dr. Phil said that?" 40/14 squinted.

"Yep. But he's unreliable. I mean, can you trust a chubby guy who writes a weight loss book? No one is gonna buy that, unless, of course, Oprah is making ya'll buy it," I laughed. They didn't. Aaah, so Oprah is involved somehow. Now we're getting somewhere.

Stretch leaned in, "Where did you say you were from?"

"Out West," I said, and continued my frontal assault, "say do you guys like Bunko?"

40/14 dropped her coffee cup, "Oh my goodness."

"I used to be more of a poker guy, but I found that drinking, cigars, gambling and guys just didn't mix. Took fifteen years of marriage before I learned that lesson, but now I'm a Bunko Man through and through."

"You play Bunko?" 40/14 was incredulous.

"Every Thursday night."

40/14 desperately sought clarification, "You mean while your wife is out for the evening?"

"No, she takes me with her, unless, of course, we're hosting. Sure it's a little awkward being the only guy. But I can see why you gals like that gosh darn game so much. What a hoot, right?"

"Uh, yeah," nodded Stretch.

These two were about to go into shock.

"So you girls all set for some shopping? Gonna melt those credit cards down to their magnetic strips? Your husbands will be disappointed if you don't. That's why we like going to work so much, so you can spend all of the money. How are we supposed to feel powerful if all the credit cards aren't maxed out? Imagine the exhilaration your husbands are going to feel when they bust open that Capital One card statement at the end of the month and read those two little magic words: over limit." I begin to tear up. "Don't let them down. Give them that joy, at least."

These yentas were now confused and concerned.

"So why are they always taking the cards away from us?" asked 40/14.

"Aww, just playing hard to get. But you knew that. There is no pleasure in keeping you from shopping, the thrill for us is watching you try to sneak all those bags from Saks into the house. Kind of a reverse psychology thing. Oh, whoops, now I'm talking out of school. You're husbands hadn't let you in on that one?"

Blank stares.

Stretch began to turn red with anger.

"I guess we're a little more liberal out West, a tad more progressive."

"I don't believe those guys. 'Have a nice trip Cathy. Shop up a storm.' If he thinks I'm going to buy a bunch of designer crap just so he can get his jollies, he's got another thing coming."

"Ooops. Guess I stepped in it there," I said.

"In that case, since it's just us girls chatting, you've probably been sold a bill of goods on the whole oral sex thing. Truth is, it's really not that big of a deal to us guys, we can take it or leave it. And, I probably shouldn't be telling you this, but with a little Pilates to stretch out and warm up, we can do it to ourselves." When you're hot you're hot. Am I the fucking man or what?

"You can do what to yourself?" 40/14 asked deliberately.

"It," I say.

"Really?" 40/14 gasped.

Stretch acted as if she hadn't heard me correctly, "It? You can do it to yourself?"

"Yeah. And, no offense, but we do it a lot better than you guys can, 'cause, you know, we've got the equipment and you don't and all that. Frankly, it's a little annoying the way you women give H-E-A-D," I whispered.

"Annoying? My husband always acts like I'm driving him insane," 40/14 counters.

I nodded intently, "Yes, well, how often do you pleasure him in that way?"

"On his birthday."

"Every single birthday?" I gasped.

"Maybe more like every other birthday, I guess," she replied.

"Okay, there you go, how hard do you think it would be to fake it for five minutes, five times a decade? Not too hard, trust me on that one. You want to call him out? Catch the rat bastard faking it. Try going down, uh, pleasing him, three, four times a week and see if he can keep up his 'Oh, baby I can't believe how good that feels' act. Like when Meg Ryan fakes an orgasm in "When Harry Met Sally." But can your guy keep it up for a month? Maybe, but when he slips up it will be the ultimate bust, he'll go a hundred thousand points in the hole. You'll own his sorry ass forever."

40/14's eyebrows arch with determination, "Maybe I'll do that."

"Stan is such a little fraud, he's always begging for it," Stretch said.

"Does begging work?" I asked.

"No, of course, not."

"Exactly," I smiled.

They just gaped, wide eyed.

"Think your husbands don't know that? Stan probably begs you to smoke him right after he's done himself. He knows he can't perform just then and he's making sure you won't ask him to."

Stretch was outraged, "We've been had. They've been playing us this whole time."

I shook my head and stared at the floor, "Don't say anything to your guys, I probably shouldn't be giving away trade secrets like that. Some men wouldn't understand."

"That's okay, you did the right thing," said Stretch.

40/14 patted me on the hand, "Your wife is a lucky woman, you are a real prince."

Ain't that the fucking truth? My work here is done. As I excused myself, the ladies whipped out their cell phones to check in with their husbands. I could feel the joy drain from their "lost weekend." They were now on a mission, a misguided mission, to "reclaim supremacy" in their relationships by cutting up their credit cards and sucking dick. I strolled to the lobby, smiling at this first blow (pardon the pun) struck for the revolution. For the rest of their married lives, two mutton heads in suburban Philadelphia would be thanking the "mysterious stranger at the St. Regis" who changed their lives forever. Their wives were going to come home, hand over their credit cards, swear off shopping and perform more fellatio than any two suburban housewives ever had. The more these guys "pretended" to enjoy it – the more dedicated their wives efforts will become. Finally, when these chicks realize how much pleasure they are actually giving their men, their icy hearts would melt and they'd all live happily ever after. The history books might even remember Stretch and 40/14 the way we do Betsy Ross, Helen Gurley Brown and Farrah Fawcett-Majors. Stretch and 40/14 will be remembered by sexually satisfied husbands everywhere as brave trailblazers who selflessly renounced the unfair world of female domination, dropped to their knees and ushered in a new era in male/female relations.

Am I being naïve? Probably. But these two weak minded simps were easily turned. Our resistance could stay underground and conduct small guerilla operations like I did at the St. Regis. If I could get a few guys working with me and we stayed under radar, our new men's movement could spread like a virus.

August 30, 2003

Finally hooked up with my brother Robbie. What a blast seeing him, it'd been almost two years. I'd been so wrapped up in Internet world I hadn't made time to visit him. I pretended it hadn't been that long and he pretended not to mind. After ten minutes together, it was like no time had passed anyway. Don't you love brothers? We haven't laid eyes on each other in forever and day and in ten minutes we're reliving the Van Halen vs. Van Hagar argument. A fun argument really, because we both take the David Lee Roth side in that argument. When Dave, with his humor and flamboyant showmanship, was unceremoniously dismissed from the band, Van Halen became boring. The greatest crime a rock band can perpetuate against humanity is to be boring. Be disgusting, be outrageous, be shocking, be stupid, be too loud, be derivative, be repetitive (AC/DC has been making the same album over and over since 1974 and they all ROCK) – just don't be boring. Sure Van Halen had some huge hits with Sammy Hagar (for the record, as a solo artist the Red Rocker kicks surprising quantities of ass), but they were BORING hits. Mostly pussy songs if you want to get technical about it. Besides, look at the masses, they can't be trusted – look at all those men out there who don't even know that their wives have enslaved them. Seems to me, Van Halen's post David Lee Roth success is further proof of the stay at home wives conspiracy.

"What's new?" Robbie asked and he got an earful. As I laid out my stay at home wives conspiracy theory to my flesh and blood, he quietly nodded in understanding. He's been married for seven years and has a three year old girl, Elena. His wife Maria was a rising star in the publishing world – until they got married. She tinkered with a novel for a couple of years, then had Elena and she's now in full-on housewife mode. Robbie, a copyright lawyer, busts his ass daily to pay for their perfect life in Connecticut. He treks into Manhattan everyday for ten hours in the office and keeps those billable hours piling up on his commute home.

"You believe me, don't you?" I said.

"Uh, yeah. I'm with ya, bro," he nodded sadly. "Things are great with Maria, but, now that you mention it, man, there's a lot I've given up. Just easier that way. Poker with the boys isn't worth the fight and even if I'd go there's that frost that hangs in the air afterwards. It's easier not to hassle it," he said. "But once in a while, I think to myself, Mom sure got a raw deal compared to Maria and her friends."

My Mom, Dorthy, Dotsie to her friends, raised Robbie and me pretty much all by herself. My Dad left Dotsie when I was six and Robbie was four – a tough hand to be dealt in any decade. Dotsie was barely thirty years old when she had to find full time work to support her two curtain climbers. The housewives of today whip up a full lather talking about how hard it is to raise kids – try doing it while working fifty hours a week, bee-atch. Hey Starbucks junkie, put in overtime at the plant and then pop off about your "exhausting" schedule. Dotsie would probably have enjoyed hanging out at the coffee shop everyday, but she had to punch in by 6 a.m., which kinda cramped her style.

My mom didn't date much, not that I can remember anyway. I sorta remember two or three guys coming around, but none of them more than once or twice. Guess she figured she didn't need any more lousy men cluttering up her life. Keep in mind, this was the seventies in New York City, looking for Mr. Goodwrench, Saturday Night Fever, Studio 54 – it wasn't like she couldn't find action if she was so inclined. Thank goodness she decided to focus on Robbie and me. She cooked for us every night, the apartment was always neat and for God's sake, she always made sure we had clean underwear on.

Every morning she got up around five, got ready for her day, made us breakfast, packed us a lunch and always, and I mean always, kissed us before she left for work. Robbie and I would hang out and watch cartoons and then go catch the bus. Sometimes we'd eat our tuna sandwiches while we laughed at Woody Woodpecker (yeah, I actually used to think he was funny). Probably a good thing, since those tuna sandwiches would ferment for about five hours until lunchtime. Who knows what strains of E. Coli we were eating everyday. Refrigerate meat? Who bothered in the seventies? We didn't know that every single fucking thing on the planet could kill you.

My mom would descend the stairs to the street below – praying that her rusted out Chevy Impala was one, still there and two, would turn over and carry her to another delightful day swimming in the steno pool at Union Carbide. After ten hours of pure joy, she'd come home and make dinner. After dinner, she'd clean the apartment (sometimes we'd help), do a couple loads of laundry in the basement and hang clothes on the line. Usually, she'd expend her last ounce of energy kicking my slacking ass so I'd finish my homework. When her day was finally done, she'd sit in a beat up recliner, an old faux leather one with the vibrating feature, and sip a single glass of McCall's Scotch Whiskey. The chair would gently vibrate, the lights would dim slightly and our black and white RCA television would be buzzing with snow. Through the static, you could barely make out what was happening on "What's Happening?" or "Chico and the Man," but she'd sit there, sipping her whiskey, drifting away. Sometimes I'd flop on the floor writing a paper or something and she'd glance down and smile at me. It was the smile of a woman content. I'll always remember that smile. This was as good as it got for her and she managed to be all right with that. Courageous, don't you think? Compare Dotsie's life to the free pass these cul-de-sac queens have today. It's a joke. Are they content? No, they're locked in an SUV arms race. My Lexus doesn't have heated seats? Send it back. I'm forty and look my age? Better visit the plastic surgeon at the strip mall. How did this generation get so fucking self-involved?

My mom was the Last of the Mohicans – after her the moms started asking themselves, "What do I want? What will make me happy?" She made a stupid choice by getting with my Dad but she was determined not to make it worse by neglecting us. It takes two to tango, after all, and Dotsie owned up to that. I felt bad for her, she got jacked hard by my Dad. She deserved more, all Robbie and I can do at this point is make her as comfortable as possible. She's proud of us, our success, our families – we're her trophies. Because we turned out all right, she knows her sacrifice wasn't in vain. Doesn't seem like much, but I'm not a mom – it sure seems to be enough for her.

Robbie pulled into the parking lot of "Super Fitness Works," a Connecticut health club. We strolled into the juice bar at five minutes before nine.

"What's this?"

"You'll see," he said. "You want a smoothie?"

"No I don't want a smoothie."

"Don't be a pussy. Try the 'Tange-a-nana,' it's got citrus fruit and bananas and shit."

"You make it sound so good," I said.

We sat there sipping our smoothies (okay, yeah, the Tange-a-nana did taste pretty good) when I heard something ominous approaching, the syncopated sound of marching, charging feet, boy.

"Try not to make eye contact," he warned.

"What? What is that sound?"

I glanced out at the parking lot and saw them. Housewives, two dozen strong, all uniformed in designer sweats and yoga outfits, marching in formation like fucking storm troopers. Their Nike aerobic shoes slapping the pavement like Nazi jackboots hitting the cobblestone streets under the Arc de Triomphe. Their faces were frozen portraits of intensity and determination as they invaded the health club. The subtle wardrobe differences seemed to suggest different ranks among these soldiers. Was the health club their boot camp? Were the Pilates classes, the step aerobics and spinning classes preparing them for some battle to come? Seeing all these stay at home wives strut into the club, in tight formation, scared the hell out of me.

"Every morning at nine," Robbie said, "The March of the House Fraus."

"They're in killer shape," I said. "Look at all those tight butts. That spinning class must really work, huh?"

"Yeah, but you get the feeling it's not all about looking good, you know? It's about something else. It's about power."

"But why have a fighting force, they've already got us under control. I mean, they may be able to pedal a stationary bike faster and longer than me. Maybe they can lift their body weight more reps than I can, and, sure, they can touch their toes, but, in a street fight I like my chances against a five foot two inch tall cutie in Lycra stretch pants."

"I don't know if they're prepping for a street fight, but there sure as hell is something going on," Robbie said.

"That's for damn sure. Between Starbucks, Bunko and Pilates, the cul-de-sac mafia have secret meeting places all over the place. Who knows what they're up to?"

"Well, Enron for starters."

"Enron?"

"Yeah, I think the housewives are behind Enron."

"You think they're capable of something that big?"

"Sure. Do you really think the CEO of the world's largest energy company is really that brazen and reckless? What guy would be that stupid?" Robbie nodded with authority.

I played devil's advocate, "I know a lot of stupid guys. Besides, how could the housewife conspiracy reach all the way to the top of Enron?"

"Hey, dumbass, do the math, there is only one degree of separation here." Robbie waited for me to catch up.

"His wife."

"Of course, his fucking wife. She drove the CEO off the bridge baby. A house in Switzerland, a Lear jet, beachfront on the Mediterranean – that shit don't come cheap."

"And they can't touch the wife," I said.

"Damn straight."

"She probably turned investigators onto him."

"Believe it."

"And the whistle blower was a woman, right?"

"See what I'm saying? The housewives blew up Enron. The CEO felt guilty, got tired of cooking the books, whatever, but his wife wouldn't let him off the treadmill. When he started to crack under pressure, and who wouldn't, she fried him in hot oil." Robbie was rolling now.

"When is enough, enough?" I cried.

"With them, too much is never enough," he said.

Pieces of this ever expanding puzzle began to come together in my mind, forming a hideous picture. An obvious thought exploded in my mind.

"If Enron, then what about Martha Stewart?" I blurted.

"Shhhh," Robbie whispered and glanced around the snack shop, making sure we weren't being watching.

"You want to know about Martha? She's running fucking rough shod through Wall Street and some poor bastard tries to stand up to her and he gets hung out to dry. But in classic 'Bridge Over the River Kwai' form – dude falls on the plunger and tries to blow up Martha," his voice rising with passion. "But she plays the 'I'm a woman, I don't understand this whole stock market stuff' card."

"Yeah, the CEO of a multi-billion dollar company gets a free pass because she's a girl who claims she's not good 'with math and numbers and stuff.' What a crock of shit that is," I said.

"A classic case of having your cake and eating it too. Who knows how many more stories like this there are? How many men have been set up to take the fall for these housewives," asked Robbie.

"A brilliant system, really, you got to hand it to them. Hillary Clinton can be president without being elected. The wife of the WorldCom CEO can line her pockets and he's the one taking the slow boat to China. So if this conspiracy has spread beyond the housewives in our cul-de-sacs to Wall Street, then how far does it go?" I wondered.

"All the way to the top," he said ominously.

"All the way to the top? The top, top?"

My mind raced, putting the pieces together. I could tell by his grim expression what he was thinking. He was thinking the unimaginable. He was naming the unnameable. He was talking about the Godfather of the housewife mafia and at last I knew who she was. I was afraid to say the name, her name, aloud, as if speaking it would somehow conjure a rain of hell fire down on our very heads.

I checked around us to be sure no one was listening, then I leaned close to my brother and whispered the awful name, "Oprah?"

"Hell yeah, Oprah, who else could it be? She's got book clubs in every neighborhood, the Oxygen Network on every cable system, she's on TV ten times a week, she produces movies, and there isn't a celebrity on the planet who doesn't owe her a solid. And get this, her production company, Harpo – it's Oprah spelled backwards."

"What are you talking about? Harpo is a Marx Brother. O-P-R...holy shit, it is Oprah spelled backwards." The blood ran out of my head, I felt dizzy and nauseous.

It was her, it's been her all this time. Oprah is the one behind the stay at home wives conspiracy. Her rise to fame personifies the rise to power of the stay at home wives. From her humble beginnings in the early eighties as a smart, scrappy and sensitive reporter and host at a local TV station in Baltimore, to the runaway success of her syndicated talk show to her emergence as a mega-personality and media mogul. She empowered the housewives as they empowered her. Men couldn't stand to watch her show for more than ten minutes without blacking out. Her show was the electronic equivalent of the women's magazines of the seventies. And the persuasive power of television proved to be an unparalleled motivating tool – rallying housewives by the millions. All of this happening right under our noses too. We thought it was entertainment for our women, to pacify them, when in reality it was a bold and brilliant grasp for power. Real power. While the men in Washington trip over their dicks and the men on Wall Street wrestle each other for fleeting, monetary power – Oprah and her housewife minions snatched up the real power, they control the homes, the children and, therefore, the men. Oprah runs the world and we are her puppets, it seemed obvious and impossible at the same time.

"Compared to Oprah, Howard Stern, the King of All Media, is a lonely Cherokee sending smoke signals somewhere in the Badlands," Robbie said.

"What do we do?" I asked. "How do you start a revolution against that? It's like standing outside the Kremlin and yelling 'Stalin sucks ass.' If we complain about waiting in line for stale bread then Oprah will send a black limousine to drive us to Gorky Park and one of her henchmen like Diane Sawyer or Katie Couric will put a bullet in our brain."

"Don't be a pessimist. In the end communism fell, the Berlin Wall did come down. We can do this bro," he insisted.

"Yeah, tell that to the Czechs that were run over by Soviet tanks in '68."

"Every revolution has its casualties. Denial is an option, Mike. Maybe you'd rather just go along, try not to rock the boat and, if you're good, Alicia will give you permission to watch the Super Bowl and the Victoria's Secret television special. Your decision bro," Robbie said.

I knew he was right. We'd been living that way for years anyway. But the difference was, and it's a big difference, now that we knew the truth, we were choosing to live this way. Having to consciously swallow that is a bitter fucking pill. Somebody please plug me back into the Matrix.

August 31, 2003

The family reunion commenced at Uncle Fred's spectacular Connecticut estate. After the usual barrage of hugging and smooching dusty old people I barely remembered, we settled in around Uncle Fred's enormous dining room table – all sixty or so of the O'Brien clan. Once upon a time this family were a proud and hearty lot from County Cork in the south of Ireland. Now look at us. Okay, not bad I guess, but surviving poverty in Ireland is much more romantic than being wealthy and struggling with marriage problems in America. I mean, technically I'm a millionaire, what the hell do I have to bitch about? Oh, sure, I'm a prisoner in my own house. My wife has me on a leash and calls me "Jo Jo the Houseboy," but really, what kind of a gripe is that compared to my Irish forefathers whose dying words were "I'm so sick of potatoes, shouldn't we go fishing or something?"

But hey, I'm not alone at this table. Robbie is coming to terms with the stay at home wives conspiracy too – probably all the husbands have their own suspicions or theories. And look at poor Uncle Fred, slumped in that wheel chair, staring off into space, drool pooling on his lip – that poor schmo really got the short shrift.

Uncle Fred had a stroke when he was only 33. A rising star at Xerox, he was already a vice president (back when VP meant something), pulling down serious bank, rolling in stock options, when one day his brain just melted down. An embolism? A brain seizure? A stroke? The doctors were never able to diagnose exactly what happened. But he was a catatonic vegetable now, that much they were sure of.

Fortunately, disability insurance paid out big time so Aunt Gina was able to afford the best care possible for Uncle Fred. A nurse provides around the clock, in-home care so Aunt Gina hasn't had to shoulder this burden alone. Twenty years is a long time to live with a completely useless husband – I know that sounds like a set up line, but seriously this dude is truly pathetic. And while Aunt Gina could've taken the money and run, she never made a move to divorce him. I always respected her for that. If I were in her shoes I only hope I would be as noble.

As we enjoyed our meal, a stunning brunette with shining blue eyes and flowing hair bounced into the room. She was probably thirty-five but, she wore it very well and her form fitting Juicy Couture sweat suit left little to the imagination. Instinctively, my eyes followed her as my brain tried to figure out which distant cousin she could possibly be. Suddenly, she stopped at Uncle Fred, wiped the drool from his chin and wheeled him out of the room.

I leaned over to my mom, "Who the hell is she?"

"Uncle Fred's nurse."

"That's his nurse?"

"Yes, Ranelle. She's a lovely girl," she said.

I was sure my mom was mistaken, "She's the nurse that lives here?"

"Yes, she takes care of Uncle Fred. It's really a nice arrangement, especially when Gina is on one of her trips."

"Since when does Aunt Gina get to travel?" I asked.

My mom laughed, "Don't you ever listen to me?"

"Your Aunt Gina has spent time on every continent on the planet, including Antarctica. She's leaving for a month in Egypt on Tuesday," she said.

"Wow. I had no idea." I watched Ranelle and Uncle Fred roll out of the dining room...must be time for a diaper change. What a shame, all that hot young talent wasted on a complete vegetable. But I guess Ranelle knows a good deal when she sees one. Not many gigs in the nursing profession can be better than this one: she gets the run of the mansion while the lady of the house is out of the country – and gets paid for it. That has to beat paying two grand a month for a crummy, first floor studio apartment overlooking an alley. Of course, the fair Ranelle has probably wiped so much stinky ass that it ain't much of a bargain.

In a way, Aunt Gina has the ultimate stay at home wife deal. Her husband generated a ton of income and now they're living off an epic insurance settlement and mature stock dividends. Gina is loaded and goes globe trotting while Uncle Fred hangs around the mansion doing his best Commander Pike impression (remember that Star Trek episode?). Unlike most stay at home wives, Aunt Gina doesn't have to spend any energy tricking Uncle Fred into being her slave. She's free, there's no need to carry on a charade, it's all pretty neat and tidy. And from what I can remember those two used to go at it like Wolverine and Buckeye. Aunt Gina was a brilliant nag, really knew how to hurt Uncle Fred by hen pecking him in front of his family. I wouldn't be surprised if, somehow, she caused his brain to fry out. She probably used that Jedi housewife "mind scan" and left it on "full power" for too long and his brain just exploded. I've felt the power of the housewife, it could happen.

Later, Aunt Gina gave me a tour of their estate. I nodded and smiled as she showed me an amazing collection of artifacts from her world travels. I maintained a distant politeness – out of respect for my elders and out of fear of her brain melting prowess. She led me into a vast room, paneled in mahogany and there sat Uncle Fred, staring mindlessly at a mammoth flat screen television. He was gaping at a Yankees game. This freaking screen was so huge Roger Clemens looked damn near life size. When he fired a pitch, I flinched.

"Why does that girl always put on sports?" Aunt Gina walked to the console, picked up the remote and switched over to the Discovery Channel.

"Studies have shown that watching sports diminishes brain wave activity. It's like a numbing cerebral massage, rather than a stimulus," she smiled. I nodded. But I felt Uncle Fred's pain. It was a good game, Clemens had a shut out going against the hated Red Sox. Besides, what else does this poor guy have to live for? And did I mention that this TV was the coolest thing I'd ever seen? Must be a high definition set – because the image was crystal fucking clear, it was like watching the game from the tenth row.

I stood quietly as Aunt Gina spent a moment watching a documentary on the Ugandan tree monkey. Damn those monkeys have red butts. Maybe it was because the image was so clear, but those red butted monkeys were so huge, so life like – if they started throwing their shit at each other, I'm certain I would've been hit.

Aunt Gina nodded to herself, apparently deeming the nature show appropriate. She kissed Uncle Fred, "See you later sweetie."

We left him to drool at "Monkey Ass Theater."

My brother cut out early. I don't think it took his wife Maria long to have her fill of the O'Brien family scene. Who can blame her? I'm related to these people by blood and I don't really like them all that much. I surely didn't trust them enough to try and rally some support for the revolution. These whipped guys, cousins, uncles, and the like, would bring it up with their wives on the car ride home.

A DRAMATIZATION OF ONE OF MY PUSSY WHIPPED COUSINS ASKING HIS WIFE FOR PERMISSION TO JOIN THE RESISTANCE:

"Honey, Cousin Mike and some of the other guys are starting a revolution and I want to, you know, help them out," my feeble cousin Patrick would say.

"What kind of revolution?" his wife Catherine would ask.

"Uhm, one for men to, you know, one to stop the wives from being the boss of us all the time," he muttered.

"Oh, I see. You don't like me being your boss?"

"Uhm, I think maybe the idea, what the fellas are suggesting, is that we could both be bosses, you know, of each other," he stammered.

"Interesting."

"So, uhm, is it all right with you if I, you know, help them out a bit?"

"Patrick?"

"Yes, dear?"

"Shut the fuck up."

"Yes, dear."

Yeah, talking to these relatives of mine would be a waste of energy and an unnecessary security risk. These are dark, dangerous times, my strategy would have to be carefully planned and executed flawlessly.

Though the reunion dragged on, it was great to see my Mom. Though I barely spoke to her. It was fun watching her work the room. She was completely in her element, engrossed in one deep conversation after another with women I vaguely recognized from scrapbooks or black and white photos.

But I was getting pretty tired of explaining to relatives who had never met my family why they hadn't come along. And when I found myself trapped in an endless conversation with Aunt Mildred, I took solace in the thought that, sooner or later Uncle Fred's nurse would stroll through again and give my mind something to chew on.

"Gina and I are going to Egypt next week. We're going to stand on the very earth where Cleopatra stood," she beamed.

"That's super. Cleopatra is quite a lady, the face that launched a thousand ships," I smiled.

"That's Helen," Mildred corrected.

"What?"

"Of Troy. Helen's face launched a thousand ships," she said.

I slapped my forehead, trying to appear interested, "That's right."

"Gina and I have spent months in the Mediterranean."

"Poor Uncle Fred," I said.

"What do you mean?" asked Aunt Mildred.

"You and Gina are on the endless world tour and that poor guy is stuck in this house."

"Yes, it's a terrible existence, I'll admit, but he does travel occasionally," she said.

"Uncle Fred travels?"

"Frederick has the best medical assistance money can buy. He's had this nurse for over ten years and she's always looking into the latest experimental therapy techniques. A couple of times a year she'll take him to a clinic somewhere," Mildred explained.

"What, like the Mayo Clinic?"

"Well, let me think. I know he's seen specialists in Thailand, Miami and Hawaii. And I want to say an island in Texas, but that can't be right. Does Texas have islands?"

I laughed to myself, "Only South Padre Island."

"Yes, that's it," she said. "South Padre Island. None of those specialists were able to help Fred, but I think the tan makes him look more healthy."

"Yeah, a tan tends to do that."

"They even tried putting him on a boat for a week at Lake Havasu so he could breath the moist air all day and night," she said.

South Padre Island? Miami? Lake Havasu? Thailand? Hawaii? Not exactly known as hot beds of medical research.

"The nurse takes him a couple times a year, you say?"

"Usually in the spring and then again in the late fall when things get a bit gloomy around here," Mildred said.

Uh, huh. Are you thinking what I'm thinking? Ranelle is dragging her catatonic meal ticket to Spring Break every year. This bimbo is partying with college studs while poor Fred watches the tide go in and out.

I walked to Uncle Fred's TV room, determined to give Ranelle a piece of my mind. It's not fair for any man to be held captive by his woman, but poor Fred was getting abused by two women at once. At least Gina was married to him. He'd made that bed and has to lie in, er, sit in it. But this Ranelle, taking advantage of a crippled old rich guy? I thought I was going to puke.

I entered to see Roger Clemens throw the high heat past a helpless Nomar Garciaparra. The crowd roared in 5.1 surround sound. The decibel level rattled my skull (I'd have to look into that surround sound too, pretty cool). I glanced around for Ranelle, she was nowhere to be seen. I saw the remote perched on Uncle Fred's lap. Why would Ranelle leave it there? It's not like he could change the channel.

I walked over and leaned down, staring right into his vacant eyes. He was looking in the direction of the television, but his eyes didn't follow the action. He rarely blinked as he looked off into space. I must've watched him for five minutes, the only thing that moved was the tiny river of saliva flowing from the corner of his mouth down to his chin. So fucking sad.

"Uncle Fred, it's me, Mike, Dotsie's boy. Yankees are looking pretty good. I don't know how the Rocket still does it." I kneeled down to get more comfortable, but it's just plain awkward talking to a corpse with a pulse.

"Uh, so how are you doing in there? Are you really in there? I haven't been to your place since a Thanksgiving when, shit, I must've been fifteen years old or something. Only a year or two before your, uh, accident or whatever you call it. Guess Aunt Gina's done a little remodeling since then, huh? Probably better that you're a veg, living through a remodel with Aunt Gina, you guys would've killed each other," I laughed. "I remember how you and Uncle Colin would sit back and make fun of Aunt Gina and all the women. I never really got what you guys were laughing at."

A TOUCHING MEMORY FROM THANKSGIVING 1980:

Uncle Colin poked Uncle Fred and pointed at me. Uncle Fred smiled, "How old are you Michael?"

"Fourteen," I replied.

They cracked up like that was funny for some reason. "Fourteen? He's fourteen Colin. Probably waking up with a boner now, eh? Do you wake up with wood, son?"

"Uncle Fred."

"Of course you do. We all do," he laughed.

"Bet you can't wait to put your pecker in some sweet young thing," Colin added.

"Oh, yes, it's good fun, to be sure, but be careful who you poke boy," added Fred.

"I know all about VD," I said.

They laughed again. But now the laughter was tempered with sadness.

"Oh, if it were only the VD you had to worry about. VD is nothing, your wang-doodle would fall off and your troubles would end there," he said quietly.

They could see from my confusion that I had no idea what they were talking about.

"You go waving your pecker around and some sweet young thing is gonna grab a hold of it and not let go," cautioned Colin.

"You see your Auntie?" said Uncle Fred.

I glanced back at Aunt Gina, "Yeah."

"That woman had a backside carved from granite. A real foxy momma, a hot babe or whatever you kids are calling pretty girls these days. Well, I was happy to have her catch a hold of my willy and, boy, she knew what to do with it. I lost my mind, I don't mind saying," a smile crept across his face.

"I know you didn't have a father around when you were growing up, but you should know it all changes when you get married," Colin said.

"You start out thinking this sweet young thing is gonna keep that willy of yours in top shape. You think she'll take it out every morning for a run and maybe polish it with her tonsils every night. But when you're married there's no one around to stop you, no one to catch you doing it, you can do it anywhere you want," said Uncle Fred.

"You do it in the bed."

"On the floor," Colin said.

"Ever do it on a table?"

"Kitchen table, sure."

"How about on a balcony?" asked Fred.

"Sure. Ever do it hanging off the balcony?"

"Seriously?"

"Believe it."

243

"You get the point son, the possibilities are endless."

"Cool," I said.

"No, not cool," said Colin.

"Huh?"

"It's cool at first, but they're setting you up."

"It's a trap," Uncle Fred added.

"They get you hooked and then cut you off son, they cut you off clean," whispered Colin.

My blood ran cold. "They cut it off?"

"That would be less painful," Colin mused.

"No, they cut you off from sex. You don't get any more of the hot lovin' son," said Uncle Fred.

"They let you taste the full meal deal and then take it away," said Colin.

"You guys are messing with me."

"Wait until you get married, then you'll see," Uncle Fred said.

I stood over the now empty shell of my uncle, "You weren't messing with me, were you Uncle Fred? Now I get it, I've been cut off more times than I can count. And the Point System, the "Honey Do" lists, the whole stay at home wives Mafia has got me on the run. I don't know what to do. Robbie and I are starting a revolt, but I haven't figured out where to begin. It may sound crazy to you, but I'm convinced that, on some level, every guy knows what the truth is. Admitting it to ourselves, that's the hard part, right? And then what are we gonna do about it anyway? There are too many of them. The housewives are too well organized. Did you try to rebel against Aunt Gina and she put you in a wheel chair? Is that what happened Uncle Fred? Did Gina do this to you?"

Uncle Fred gazed into oblivion. I wiped the drool off his lip. In a way, he had it made. Sitting around watching sports on the best television ever, having a sexy nurse take care of your every need, and, as an added bonus your wife leaves the country for half the year. This guy never gets nagged because all he's capable of is sitting up straight. He could never screw anything up because nothing is ever expected of him. He never gets yelled at for buying the wrong kind of toilet paper. Yes, except for the part about being a human rutabaga, Uncle Fred was living the dream.

As I sat with Uncle Fred, I noticed his arms looked pretty damn good for a man who atrophied back in the eighties. I glanced around, making sure no one was watching, and gave his biceps a squeeze. I work out twice, three times a week and his arm was way more solid than my spindly biceps. Damn. I gotta get me a hot nurse physical therapist. I felt his calf muscles, they were strong and toned too – not bad for a guy sitting on his ass since Reagan's first term.

"I'm sorry Uncle Fred, sorry this happened to you. But, in a weird way, it's probably for the best. It's worse out there than you and Uncle Colin could've imagined. They've all gotten together, all the housewives, they're one big network now, Oprah gives them their marching orders. We're going to work, they're collecting the paychecks and all we get is the grief. You're better off in this chair. At least the target is off your back."

I put a hand on his shoulder and we watched the end of the Yankee game in silence. Well, I was silent, I guess he's always silent anyway. We watched as reliever Mariano Rivera blew the save opportunity by giving up a two run triple to Bill Mueller in the ninth, I felt something pass between Fred and I. The closing of a circle, a completion of the conversation we'd had over twenty years before. Now he was a fallen soldier and I felt like a fugitive on the run. The game gave way to an Ab-Roller infomercial and I switched off the amazing television.

"I'll go find Ranelle," I kissed the top of his head and started out of the room.

"Fucking Yankees," a hushed voice said.

I spun around. There was no one in the room but Fred and me...only me and Fred. Then it hit me like a safe hitting the sidewalk – Uncle Fred, you fucking rat bastard!

"What the hell?" I gasped.

"Be cool, be cool," he whispered. His lips didn't move. It was like watching a vaudeville act and Fred was both the ventriloquist and the dummy.

I came around, gaping. His eyes were clear, staring right at me. He winked. The catatonic motherfucker winked.

"You gotta be shitting me," I said.

"Why in the hell would Mariano go inside on Mueller three straight pitches? He's leading the majors, hitting what, three-forty? He thinks Mueller can't catch up to a ninety-three mile an hour fastball? Rivera is so arrogant."

I could not believe my eyes. "You're all right? There's nothing wrong with you?"

"Don't be so damn obvious. Put on PBS and stand next to me," Uncle Fred spat.

I clicked the remote. A biography of Stephen Hawking appeared on the television. Uncle Fred stared at the handicapped physicist on the giant screen.

"Look at him. Figured out the origin of the universe or some such horse shit. Both of us in wheel chairs – but I ask you, who is the genius? I go to Spring Break every fucking year with a nurse who gives me a hard on when she smiles and, here's the kicker, my wife sends me. Who is genius?" he grinned at me.

"So, the nurse is your mistress?"

"Did your mother drop you on your head as a child? You never were too quick."

"Shit. Uncle Fred, she's hotter than hell."

"No shit. Been with me for twelve years. That young gal dishes it out, and she can take it too, if you get my meaning."

"And Aunt Gina has no idea?"

"I don't think so. If she does, she doesn't care. She's happy, I'm happy. If Gina suspects, she isn't letting on. Why would she ruin a good thing? Besides, I'd never make a fool of Gina. I put on a good show for her friends and her sisters. The drooling, the crapping my drawers, staring at the wallpaper, it takes a real commitment to pull this off. But it's all worth it, trust me," he said. "There's only one drag, Ranelle isn't much for sports. I have nobody to talk sports with. That's what I miss the most. Talking sports. Some days I think I might lose my mind."

I was totally tripping, but Uncle Fred rattled on.

247

"Do you think the Yankees can go all the way? I don't know if the Rocket has the juice. And Giambi better pull that bat out of his ass, Godzilla can't do it by himself," he said.

My body slowly went numb as I completely absorbed this revelation. The dude faked... a... fucking STROKE! And kept it up for two decades plus. He decided he'd rather sit in a wheelchair drooling all day than be an enslaved husband. Unbelievable. Of course, Ranelle was a top rank hottie and I'd seen guys do risky, stupid things to get with babes like her. And his television was really, really neat. But somehow, I didn't see faking a waking coma as an option for me. That is a hell of a lot of work. And what if he gets caught?

"Uncle Fred, hang on. So what should I do?"

"What should you do?"

"Yeah, about the stay at home wives conspiracy, about my wife," I said.

"Son, I faked a massive brain embolism so I wouldn't have to deal with my wife or any more of her shit. You really think I'm the guy you should be getting advice from?"

Point taken.

September 1, 2003

I'm cruising at about 35,000 feet, heading West on some United Airlines flight, unfortunately, not the one I was scheduled on. Last night I was a bit demoralized after leaving Uncle Fred's and decided to plant myself in the St. Regis bar and undergo alcohol therapy. In times of trouble I've been known to seek the experienced counsel of Jack Daniels and Jim Beam.

The boys and I were deep in thought and making terrific progress when this skinny, pretty blonde sits at the bar a few stools down. She looked to be mid-thirties, with a plain, short Meg Ryan hair cut, and she had the most gorgeous green eyes. Jack and Jim had slowed my reflexes and she totally busted me checking her out. But instead of getting pissed or telling me to fuck off, she stared at me. I smiled back.

Finally, she spoke, "Mike?"

I looked at the bartender, confused. He pointed at the blonde. I tried to focus on her.

"Mike O'Brien? Is that you? It's me. Lisa, Lisa Caudill," she smiled. I knew it was her because I felt electricity pulse through me when she said her name.

Lisa Caudill? You've got to be cranking me. I haven't seen her since graduation, when she cried on my shoulder one last time over Larry the stumbling, demented man-child.

"Lisa? I must be really hammered," I mumbled.

She moved to the stool next to me. "You may be hammered, but it's still me." She laughed and kissed me on the cheek.

We talked and drank for a couple hours, getting caught up on life. Lisa had made a nice career in public relations, but things had never really taken off like they should've for someone like her.

"I can't believe you never got married. You were the best catch on the entire campus, in the entire Willamette Valley."

"Says you," she smiled reluctantly. "You were always so sweet to me. When I was young, I definitely took 'sweet' for granted."

Embarrassed, I immediately knocked over my Jack and Coke. "I played golf with Larry the other day," I blurted.

"Speaking of assholes, how is he?" she laughed.

"He lives everyday with his nuts in a blender. After he broke up with you he should've shot himself in the head. Hell, I almost shot him myself."

Lisa smiled, staring right into me.

"Are you happy?"

"Yeah. I'm really glad I ran into you."

"No, I mean are you happy with your life?"

I downed another Jack and Coke, "Not a good week to ask me that."

"You deserve to be happy," she said. "You're a good person. If anyone should be happy it's you."

"What about you? Are you happy?" I asked.

"Not a good decade to ask me that," she smiled.

"You managed to avoid falling in with the housewife mafia, that's something."

"I'm not gonna lie to you Mike, we go back too far. They tried to recruit me."

"They did?"

"Yes. They even helped me pick out a guy, a Wall Street broker. He was loaded, handsome and had no idea he was being targeted."

"Really? They really do that?" I asked.

"That and much more."

"So what happened?"

"I couldn't do it," she said. "If I married him, I'd be burying every dream I'd ever had. I'd always dreamt of having a man love me and treat me like his princess. I didn't want to sucker some guy in, trap him. I wanted to be adored. I wanted to run my own public relations firm, be a success on my own terms, not just piggy back off his career. Bottom line, I guess I didn't want to be a stay at home wife."

I knocked back another Jack and Coke. Lisa had confirmed everything I had come to know. Of course, I was totally drunk off my ass, but that was beside the point.

"I knew it. I knew it," I slurred.

She put her hand on mine, "I'm sorry Mike."

I looked into her green eyes. Even after all these years, Lisa was still the most beautiful woman I'd ever laid eyes on. The years had worn on her a little, but her spirit was still kicking. I know I was looking at her through nostalgia goggles, but she was magical – she always had been.

"I have to tell you something Mike," she smiled. "When I was engaged to Christof –"

"Christof?"

"Yeah, I know, it only sounds gay. With Christof I kept wondering what I would have to do to make him look at me the way you used to. I wondered if it was possible to do things or say things to make him want me, love me? And if I could make him feel that way could it ever be like the real thing? I knew he'd never look at me like I was the most wonderful girl in the world. That's how you looked at me." She lit up the room with her smile, again. "I knew it couldn't be Christof. Anyway, I guess you saved me from making the mistake of my life." She leaned in and kissed me. Instinctively, and for old times sake, I gave her my cheek, but she grabbed my face with both hands and our lips melted together.

Next thing I remember we're on a bed rolling around, it's my room I think. Clothes are flying. Her sweet skin is pressing against me. Her gorgeous lips locked on mine.

"You loved me then, didn't you?" she asked breathlessly.

"You know I did."

She kissed me hard again – it was magnificent.

"Do you think you could love me again?"

That question should've been an easy one. The babe that has been wandering around my brain, killing time since college, was about to give me something I'd dreamed of since my freshman year – her. I should've said "yes" and begun my new life with the first woman I ever loved. But then I thought of Alicia. Dammit, my wife is always fucking everything up for me.

Right about now Fate is getting pretty fucking pissed off at me. One minute I'm alone in the St. Regis bar getting plowed and Fate delivers Lisa Caudill out of the blue. And what do I say to Fate? "Thanks, but no thanks."

What do I say to Lisa? "I'm sorry."

Lisa nods and flops back onto a stack of pillows. "Twenty years too late, huh? I'm a little slow on the up take," she smiles. She kisses my neck and squeezes me tight. "At least we can have a little fun tonight, right? I owe you that much."

Now, if you ever meet me, feel free to kick my ass – but I kissed Lisa on the cheek and crawled off the bed. She sat there in her bra and panties – those sexy, sheer Victoria's Secret bra and panties too. Fuck, couldn't I have waited until she at least took off her bra? Haven't I been dreaming about those spectacular globes of hers for my entire adult life? My conscience, it couldn't come at a worse time.

I guess I still love Alicia. I can't be the one to let that deal go down. I'll take on the whole housewife mafia. I'll hunt down Oprah if I have to. Martha Stewart? Bring her on. Rosie O'Donnell in a steel cage death match? Fine. I'll go mano a mano with Jane Fonda – I have no fear.

Lisa smiled sadly, her green eyes piercing my soul, "Your wife is a lucky woman."

"Could I ask you something?"

"Sure, Mike."

"Can I see your tits? Just for a second?"

Lisa broke into a big smile, "You know what I think?"

"What?"

"I think you're really drunk," she said.

That was the last thing I remember. I woke up in my room, alone, fully dressed, late for my flight. No note from Lisa, I don't even know if she stayed over. Funny, thing too, the bed was made. I don't remember doing it. Did Lisa make it? Had housekeeping been here? And now I'm fully dressed. My clothes smelled of smoke and whiskey, but not of Lisa's heavenly perfume. How fucking drunk was I? Had Lisa even been here at all?

I had to "de-plane" in Chicago for a two hour layover, which worked out great because I had a world class hangover. I was killing time browsing at a newsstand when an "O" magazine caught my eye. As I looked at the "O" on the cover, the logo began to twist and spin, hypnotizing me, drawing me closer. Next thing I know, I'm laying down my five bucks for Oprah's magazine. Perhaps my subconscious had seen this propaganda tool of the enemy as an olive branch to my wife. I walked back into the concourse wondering why I'd spent money to fill the stay at home wives war chest, when Fate intervened again: there, in the concourse, surrounded by a half dozen minions was the Queen of the World herself, Oprah Winfrey.

My mind swirled as I stepped boldly toward her. With each step I drew closer to a decision that would affect the rest of my life. Here was a chance to take out the Godfather herself. Lop off the head of the beast and the body is useless. Dark thoughts danced through my brain, thoughts that had probably visited John Hinckley, Mark David Chapman and Lee Harvey Oswald. As I reached the edge of her circle, she glanced at me with a bemused, curious look. I moved closer, coiled, poised to strike. Then something inexplicable happened.

"Hi Oprah, I hate to bother you, but my wife's a big fan. Could I trouble you for an autograph?"

I smiled blankly.

"Sure," I handed her the magazine.

"What's her name?"

"Alicia," I said without hesitation.

"And what's your name?" she asked.

I hesitated. If I gave up my name would I be betrayed by some kind of super-secret-housewife background check? Would she know I had infiltrated my neighborhood stay at home wives chapter? Had she been in direct contact with Alicia? Had Oprah given the order to donate my couch to the Salvation Army?

"It's just a little thing, I do. First name is fine," she repeated.

"Oh, sorry, yeah, it's Mike."

She quickly scrawled something on the cover with a silver metallic marker and handed me back the magazine.

"Thank you Oprah, you're the best" I gushed. She nodded and moved on to the next person. I stepped back, feeling a little light headed. I sat down on the edge of a planter and examined the "O" magazine.

Here's what she wrote:

"To Alicia,

Thanks for being there. Keep Mike happy – he's good people.

Love, Oprah"

Keep Mike happy? He's good people? This was not what I expected from the leader of the stay at home wives conspiracy. I broke out in a cold sweat. Something wasn't right. I called my brother Robbie on my cell.

"Hello?"

"Robbie. It's not Oprah."

"What? Are you calling from a secure line?"

"Oprah's not behind the conspiracy."

"What are you talking about? Of course she is," he protested.

"I'm at O'Hare right now, Oprah just autographed an "O" magazine for me."

"You bought an "O" magazine? What are you thinking? Have you lost –"

"Listen to me, it's not her. She wrote: 'To Alicia, Thanks for being there. Keep Mike happy – he's good people. Love, Oprah'. See, it's not her. If she were the Godfather, why would she write that?"

There was silence on the other end.

"Robbie?"

"Star fucker."

"What?"

"You met a celebrity and you lost your mind. You always do," he said.

"I always do? What do you mean I always do? How many celebrities have I met?" I protested.

"Well, there's Oprah here...and Ted Nugent."

"Hey, that's not fair. That was a totally different scenario, Terrible Ted is an icon, man, 'Wango Tango?' 'Great White Buffalo?' 'Cat Scratch Fever?' Who wouldn't puke when meeting him? Besides Oprah isn't even a housewife," I said.

"She is too," Robbie retorted.

"No, she's not."

"She isn't? What about Steadman?"

"He's her boyfriend, significant other or something. I'm not even sure if they live together."

"Oh." Robbie went silent, apparently deep in thought.

"If you think about it Oprah is the furthest thing from your average stay at home wife. She works like ten jobs. She is a TV host, a producer, an actress, a columnist, a publisher, a philanthropist – I'm not backsliding here, but Oprah does a lot of good for a lot of people with that show of hers and her charities."

More silence.

"Robbie?"

"I'm thinking."

"If she was the Godfather, why would she sign my magazine Robbie? Why would she encourage Alicia to keep me happy? There is no doubt in my mind that these house-wives are banded together. The housewives of America are making a concerted and collected effort to have their cake and eat it too, I'm convinced of that. But, Oprah isn't calling the shots from Chicago," I said. "And how would you keep a single leader, the head of an organized chain of command, a total secret? It would be impossible."

"I don't know. Women are better at secrets than men are. If anyone could do it, these housewives could."

"No way. I looked Oprah square in the eye. Sure it was kinda exciting to meet her, but there is no way she's some malevolent kingpin."

Robbie paused again.

"Robbie? You still there?"

"Jane Fonda," he said.

"What?"

"You're right, it's not Oprah, it's Jane Fonda – she's their leader."

"You think?"

"Remember those house fraus goose stepping into that health club?"

"I'll never forget the horror," I said.

"Who were they dressed like? Who popularized aerobics in the eighties with her subversive workout videos? Who married the richest guy in America only to divorce him and take his money?"

"That's right, I forgot about Ted Turner, poor bastard," I gasped.

"Fonda suckered in the men by taking naked in "Barbarella." We didn't see her as a threat and then she single handedly starts the whole chick flick revolution, 'Electric Horseman?' 'Coming Home?' 'On Golden Pond?' 'Coal Miner's Daughter?' "

Okay, 'Coal Miner's Daughter' was Sissy Spacek but why stop him when he's on a roll?

"Jane Fonda blazed the trail for the likes of 'An Officer and a Gentleman,' 'Beaches,' 'You've Got Mail,' 'Sleepless In Seattle" and 'Erin Fucking Brockovich.' She turned the multiplex into a torture chamber for anyone with balls."

"I thought Albert Finney was pretty good in 'Erin Brockovich'," I said.

Robbie pressed on, "Yes, old 'Hanoi Jane' has been working at this for decades, right under our noses too. I'll bet the Russians trained her in subversive propaganda techniques when she was working with the Viet Cong. This also explains why her brother Peter Fonda is such a stoner," he said.

"It does?"

"If your sister were the anti-Christ wouldn't you be self-medicating all the time too? It's Jane Fonda. Why didn't I see it before?"

"Hey Robbie, how many points do you think an autograph from Oprah is worth anyway? I'm gonna score big with Alicia, right?"

"Sell out," he said and hung up.

September 3, 2003

I rolled into the Portland International Airport none the worse for wear, because, I guess, I couldn't get any more worse for wear...you know what I mean.

I ducked into the Starbucks off the C concourse. A barista chirped, "What can I get you for?" I was stunned – it was my missing punky barista.

"You're okay?" I stammered.

"Yeah, I'm fine, these early mornings do suck, but I'm fine, thanks," she said, not recognizing me. "What can I make for you?"

Had they wiped her mind clean, no memories, no bad thoughts? I proceeded with caution, "You used to work at the Starbucks on Barnes Road, right?"

She studied me for a minute then a glimmer of recognition crossed her face, "Yeah. Oh, yeah, I know you. You were like the only guy who ever came into that place who wasn't scared. Those bitchy housewives almost drove me to suicide," she laughed. "And that manager was no rave either. Cranky."

"So you..."

"So I asked for a transfer to another store and here I am."

"You weren't 'disappeared' then?"

"Huh?"

"Nothing."

"The airport is great. Everybody's going somewhere. Each day is different. That other neighborhood, man, it's like "Ground Hog's Day" crossed with "The Stepford Wives," everyday is identical and all those housewives look the same. No offense, but I don't know how you can stand to live there. I almost went insane and I only worked there."

September 4, 2003

Let's recap: Oprah's not the evil, all knowing Puppet Master, the housewife syndicate didn't bury my punky barista in a landfill, my encounter with Lisa Caudill was probably a drunken hallucination, and my brother the conspiracy nut is scaring me a little and finally, I hate flying on the red eye. There's always one guy wheezing, keeping everyone else awake. I need to sleep before I can sort things out.

I stepped out of my cab, into my house and walked in on...you guessed it, a Botox party. The living room was packed. Alicia and ten stay at home wives from the local chapter including Debra (she of the new car), Kristen (Larry's wife), Susie (Jim's wife) and that chick that always wears the purple suit at the pool (why can't I ever remember her name...Melinda). And flitting about the room, wielding a giant needle, was a gorgeous, petite Frankenstein in a white lab coat. This wannabe plastic surgeon had Angelina Jolie's lips, Kim Cattral's cheekbones, Denise Richards' nose and Alyssa Milano's tits. When she smiled, I swear it looked like a dog snarling. Nothing on her whole face moved, not her forehead or her cheeks – she just bared her fangs. Couldn't quite place the teeth, they could've been Sarah Jessica Parker's or maybe Jessica Biel's.

The cold frost coming from twelve pairs of squinting eyeballs hit me like an avalanche.

"Uh, hi honey, I'm home," I forced a smile and retreated.

Alicia met me at the stairs with the news, "I didn't know you'd be back today. I meant to call you. We have to talk."

"Here I am."

"Not with the girls here."

"Alicia. Talk. It's okay."

"Okay," she took a deep, theatrical breath, "I think we should take a little time apart."

"I've been gone a week. Isn't that a little time?"

"This is why I didn't want to talk now."

I couldn't believe what I was hearing, "This isn't you talking."

"What does that mean?"

"I mean you're acting like a parrot. Those yentas in there say it and you repeat it. I married you Alicia, not the whole damn neighborhood."

"I'm not doing this now," she headed back to the party.

"Alicia?"

"What?" She didn't turn around.

"Don't get that stuff shot into your face. It looks freaky, like you're wearing a mask or something. You're a hot mom in her thirties. Be happy with that. I am."

She shook her head and disappeared.

September 5, 2003

After Alicia kicked me out last night things got a little crazy.

I called Doctor Robert to see if I could crash out in his guest house.

"You know, Mike, it's not really a good time," he said.

"No shit Sherlock, why do you think I'm calling?"

"I understand, it's just that Jill – "

"Jill? Is she listening in on the kitchen phone? Are you sending her hand signals? I'm asking you, dude," my voice rose.

"Jill invited over some, uh, friends, she met on the Internet. We've actually got a full house right now. I'm sorry Mike," Doctor Robert said.

"Hey, I understand, I'm breaking down over here, but far be it from me to crash your little Crisco party."

I hung up the phone. Jill had to be the craziest Mormon I've ever met. Note to self to search the Internet for video of their little party, 'cause you never make a friend on the Internet without somebody showing up with a fucking camcorder.

Next I called Jim. Susie was at my house getting shit pumped into her face through a fucking needle so it shouldn't be a big deal to sneak into his guest room and sleep off my jet lag before she even finds out I'm there. But the pussy wouldn't pick up. Reverting to my true stalker nature I called him like sixteen times in three minutes:

- "Jim, its Mike, need a favor. Pick up bud. Pick up." Click.

- I dialed again, "Maybe you're in the shitter or something, call me on my cell. It's Mike."
- A few seconds later, "Cut it clean off already and pick up the damn phone, dude." Click.
- "Hey Jimbo, it's Mike again. Are you screening your calls you chiseler? I'm on my cell. I think I told you that already. I'm back in town and need to talk to you." Click.
- I hit speed dial, "Jim, I know that Susie isn't home. Pick up the phone you son-of-a-bitch. Alicia threw me out and I need to crash at your place," my tone grew sharper. "Pick up already." Click.
- "Listen fuckstick, I know you're home with the kids. Where else would you be you big weenus? Your wife is out spending hundreds, maybe thousands of your hard earned dollars making her lips look like you punched her, but don't pick up and talk to bad Mike, the scourge of the neighborhood." Click.
- The phone went to voice mail without a ring, I'll have to give it an extra second between calls next time. "Sorry about calling you a fuckstick…but I meant the weenus part. I could use a friend here, you don't have to be afraid of your wife, we can all rally together and turn this whole thing around. We just need a couple guys to get it started."
- I waited almost a full minute before redialing. "Listen, I really don't like talking on the phone anyway, so I'm just going to come over."

A voice was suddenly on the other end, "Bad idea Mike."

"Jim? What the hell, you are home."

"Sorry dude, you're putting me in a spot here. I'm not allowed to talk with you and Susie checks the phone records." He truly sounded nervous.

"Are you shitting me here Jim? It's time to say enough is enough."

"Okay, enough is enough." The phone went dead.

"Un-fucking-believable," I muttered to myself.

Next I tried Larry.

A sweet, vaguely foreign voice said "Hello?"

"Uh, hi, is Larry home?" I asked.

"No, he still at the working. A big meeting with the people tonight," the nanny replied.

Working late, huh?

Def Leppard's "Pour Some Sugar On Me" blared at face melting decibels. I was only grateful the Stars management was rigorously enforcing my Guns 'N Roses ban. If Axl ever gets off his psychotic ass and releases *Chinese Democracy* maybe I'll put in a good word for him. Of course, allowing the strippers to dance to Def Leppard was every bit as heinous as Guns 'N Roses. Though, I had to admit the cheesy dramatics of "Pyromaniac," "Photograph" and "Hysteria" did lend themselves to hanging from the brass pole, dry humping the stage and nude handstands.

I found Larry in his booth, sucking on a ten dollar Pepsi and trying to get the attention of a lanky blonde with glowing blue eye shadow. They might as well put a brass sign on that booth with Larry's name on it. I wonder if Stars has thought of selling seat franchises?

Larry seemed glad to see me, "Mike, hey buddy, have a seat man. Let me get you a drink and a set of double Ds." He thought this was hysterically funny. Odd, since he wasn't drunk. "Aww, come on man, so she threw you out. You'll live."

"How did you know that?"

"Know what?"

"Know that Alicia threw me out, dumbfuck," I shouted.

"Don't call me "dumbfuck," you're the asshole that got himself booted out of his mansion...dumbfuck," Larry retorted.

I tried to calm down, "Larry, I landed in Portland an hour ago, I just saw Alicia, did Kristen tell you this was going to happen?"

"Yeah, of course. Those two talk all the time. She said Alicia felt like a little time –"

"Apart would be good for us," I finished the sentence for him.

"It's probably for the best," he patted me on the back.

"How's that?"

"Now I don't have to hang out at Stars alone. The babes are totally going to dig you. Oh, and the hottie from the golf course, your caddy is around here somewhere. She was asking about you," he said.

The Def Leppard triple shot concluded, the dancer collected her outfit off the stage in a series of cat like lunges. Larry walked over and threw a hand full of singles on the stage for her.

"Like the new moves Crystal, you been taking dance classes?" smiled Larry.

The skinny brunette with fake tits that were two sizes too large beamed like it was Christmas. "Yeah, I have Larry. Can you really tell?"

He smiled shyly, "You move like a figure skater, all graceful and everything." Go for it Shakespeare.

"Thanks sweetie. Want a couch dance?" Crystal smiled again, trying to close the deal.

"Sure thing," said Larry.

She lit up again. Does life get any fucking better?

"Give me a minute to get my clothes on," I heard her shout.

"What's the point of that?" I wondered aloud.

Larry walked back to get his Pepsi, "This thing is like a passport. They see you without a drink, they'll bring you another one at ten bucks a pop."

"Larry, we can't let the housewives run us into the ground," I blurted.

He smiled sadly, as if to say, "You pathetic idiot, don't you get it yet?"

"Listen to me. We can form a wedge to divide and disrupt their housewife activities. We'll get another guy and make a three pronged wedge. I guess with three prongs, it'd be more like a pitchfork. Whaddaya say Larry, wanna form a pitchfork?"

Metallica rocked the house and I'm not sure how much Larry could actually hear. He nodded a couple times and then his eyes wandered to a dirty blonde dancer hanging upside down on a brass pole, finally, he said "What the fuck are you talking about?"

"Larry, you're with me right?"

"Why are you always trying to make waves?" was all he said.

"Is this it? Are we really going to going to sit back and get worked by our wives for the rest of our lives," I said.

"So we should become a pitchfork? What does that even mean?" Larry asked.

"Okay. What if we all went on strike? We quit working, we cut them off from the cash. We take out their legs."

"Easy for you to say, you don't have to work," said Larry.

"Don't get hung up on the details. Try to grasp the concept," I said.

Larry craned his head sideways as the dancer, in an impressive, gravity-defying feat, extended herself horizontally off the pole.

"If the sink starts leaking, don't fix it," I said.

"Kristen will call a plumber," Larry replied.

"Not if you've cut her off from the money, dude. She'll have to come to you and barter with you. I'm telling you we can get in on this whole Point System thing. 'Honey, you want the sink fixed? Fine. You'll have to make out with me like we're two teenagers at the drive-in.' And she'll have to enjoy it or it doesn't count."

"That's stupid. Kristen would never go for that," Larry said.

"She doesn't have to agree to it, man. Just do it – and if we all are doing it, she won't have any choice."

Larry glanced at his watch, "Is it really one thirty already?"

I squinted at my watch, "More like ten 'til two."

"I'm a dead man," said Larry.

"Come on dude, no show-no call. This is your chance to stick it to her, to show her who is boss, to reclaim your rightful place on the throne. Come on dude, let's pull an all nighter."

"Easy for you to say, you don't have any place to go," he said.

Okay, that one hurt but I'm not going down without a fight, "Larry, show her that you can do whatever you want."

"But I can't. I'm married and have kids," he said.

"And your wife has your balls in a porcelain jar on the mantle," I said.

"Okay, fine. Kristen has my balls. So what?"

"So what? So she takes them out in front of her friends and dances the Macarena on them. She doesn't respect you, man. She takes pride in owning your sorry ass," I shook my head in contempt.

"You'd be wise to accept your situation and deal with it. Otherwise it will drive you crazy or, worse, you'll be a weekend dad for the rest of your life," Larry said.

"I would accept my situation, except, unlike you, I'm not a fucking pussy."

"Kristen says if you don't watch your step Alicia is gonna hire the nastiest shark eating bastard lawyer and take you for everything," he said.

"Don't you quote your demonic bitch wife to me," I slammed my ten dollar Pepsi on the table. "It's your wife, all the wives that are filling Alicia's head with shit in the first place. Tell Kristen to shut up and mind her own fucking business. She's a damn gossip. She's running around like this is high school," I yelled. "Tell her to butt out of my life," I warned.

"Alright, Mike. Settle down." Larry put his fat paw on my shoulder. I took a deep breath and sat back down.

"We all deal in the best way we know how. There are ways to side step these control issues. Your wife can only bust your chops when you're at home, right? And she needs money so she can hang out at the pool with her girlfriends all day. You said yourself that we're the life blood of their operation, right? So go get yourself a job. Some boring corporate thing that you can sleepwalk through and spend your days playing golf and fucking off. If she calls you at the office ten times a day, you don't have to talk to her – be in a meeting. That way she can't give you a big "to do" list. And, of course, you'll probably have to 'work late' at your new job. Of course, the "working late" bit requires an office mate to back you up with an alibi, 'yeah, he's around here somewhere, I think he went up to design to pick up some samples.' But that's good for two hours a night, easy." Larry slapped the table happily. Ta-da, there it is, the key to happiness. Lying like a fourth grader who showed his pee-pee to the girls at recess.

"Two hours a night in this dark place?" I asked. "What kind of life is that?"

"Hello? Naked chicks," Larry laughed, "What the fuck, Mike?"

"Larry, Kristen's broken you in half you sad son-of-a-bitch and now she's making sure Alicia and I can't be happy either," I said.

"You want to blame your problems on my wife? Fuck off," Larry laughed and turned his attention back to the main stage.

"You've made it so easy for her to run your house, now she wants to run everyone else's," I said. "You're a freaking regular at Stars dude. Every girl knows you by name. Has Randy given you a key to the place yet?" I'm a bastard, I know.

"Mike...you suck," he stammered.

His skinny brunette emerged from behind a velvet curtain; her eyes searched the club for her knight in shining armor. I watched her face brighten when she saw Larry. I nodded in her direction, Larry turned and waved to her. He slid out of the booth.

"Have fun," I managed.

Larry looked back like he wanted to say something. He didn't. He left me sitting in his booth, guarding his ten dollar Pepsi.

"Hi honey, would you like a table dance?"

I looked up to see Sandi, er, Amaretto, you know, my caddy.

She smiled when she recognized me, "Hey you finally came to see me?"

"Well, uh, yeah, it's been too long. My golf game is sucking big time. We may need to go play 54 holes in Hawaii or something," I improvised.

"Ah, you're just talking shit."

"No seriously, my golf game is sucking big time," I laughed. Sandi laughed and her boobs jiggled, yeah, I remember that, a very endearing trait.

We retired to the VIP suite with a couple of bottles of champagne. I eased back on the leather couch in a "room" basically made out of drapes. Every so often a bouncer would stick his head in to make sure Sandi wasn't riding me bareback or something. Like Chris Rock says, "no matter what anyone says, there is no sex in the champagne suite."

As it turns out there was more talking than dancing, Sandi was an amazing, attentive listener. I don't know if Sandi was so sweet because I was hemorrhaging cash like a dot com start up in a Third World country, but I really felt like I could open up with her. Maybe it was because she was mostly naked, but she seemed to be totally open and honest, she wasn't putting on an act (okay, except for the music, the lights, the costume and the stage name). Maybe being behind the veil of the velvet drapes of the VIP suite reminded me of a confessional booth or maybe I was drunk on cheap champagne, whatever, I talked this poor girl half to death. After the first couple of songs, she put her top back on and sat down next to me and listened to my epic tale of woe. I told her everything I could remember about the Stay at Home Wives Conspiracy. I told her about the Witches Lair at the pool, the Starbucks meeting post, the Thursday night Bunko game, Alicia's new Mercedes, the Point System, being Cut Off, the Nazi Snore tactics, the Honey Do lists, the yentas at the St. Regis, the March of the House Fraus and even that Jane Fonda was controlling the whole operation from behind the scenes. Sandi didn't buy that one, Oprah made more sense to her than Jane Fonda.

I shook my head, "It's not Oprah. If you met her you'd agree with me. Very warm, giving, a sweet woman and a real talent," I slurred.

Sandi was impressed, "You know Oprah?"

"Yeah, we're friends, more like acquaintances really, but sure, I just saw Oprah when I was in Chicago," I said.

"You are a real mover and shaker," she purred. Then she sat up straight, a light bulb went off, "If I had to pick one person, I'd say it was Jennifer Aniston."

"Jennifer Aniston? From "Friends"?" I laughed.

"What? She went out and snagged the most eligible bachelor on the planet, didn't she? Every time she changes her hairstyle she's on the cover of a bazillion magazines. She has major influence. Her show is on five times a day in every city in the country, so everyone knows who she is. Plus she's really sweet, no one would ever expect that Jennifer Aniston was the Stay at Home Wives anti-Christ. Let's wait and see what happens when she is done with "Friends." She'll have more free time on her hands, that's when she's going to make her move. Just you watch," she nodded emphatically.

She finished off the last bottle of champagne and leaned right up to me until our noses touched, "Let's get out of here," she grinned.

I ended up back at Sandi's Sellwood condo that she shares with Darcy, a lanky blonde dancer covered with tattoos. The place was neat and clean. She had bought the place as an investment a couple years back and after she had trouble keeping it rented out, decided to move in herself. This kid was more together than you'd expect someone who takes off their clothes for a living to be. What was I doing here? What did she see in me? I'm not sure. Maybe she went for the paranoid-delusional-married, going on forty-millionaire with a Porsche-type.

We had a couple beers and talked more, about me. Fuck, could I be any more self-involved? Sandi's advice to me? Put things back together with Alicia, regardless. She was my wife, we had made a commitment to each other, stand by it.

"For better or worse," Sandi said, "You guys did that part in your vows, right?"

"Yeah."

"Then quit over thinking it Mike. It may not be the perfect situation, but it's not that complicated. Maybe these housewives are out to get you, out to control all men – and trust me if a woman wanted to control a man it ain't all that hard. But if you let them push you out of that life, you'll still have to start up a whole new one. And for all the effort that's gonna take, who's to say the new life is going to be any better? Put that energy into saving the life you have."

Wow. I'm either really drunk or she's pretty smart, some uncanny wisdom from a stripper – if we ever have the Male Equality Revolution Sandi could be our Dr. Phil. She gave me a big hug, one of those good, soul affirming hugs. We held each other for a moment, then Sandi looked deep into my eyes, "So, you wanna have a threesome with me and Darcy, or what?"

I swallowed my tongue. I guess a look of shock registered on my tired, drunk face.

"What? Didn't you know all that self disclosure and emotional intimacy was making me horny?"

"I, uh…"

"Look, Mike, I'm happy to help you straighten out your goofed up little life, but I gotta get laid over here."

She led me into the bedroom where Darcy lay spread eagle on the bed, nude. Somehow she had managed to handcuff her wrists and ankles to the bedposts.

"This is Darcy."

"Uh, hi Darcy, nice to meet you, " I stuttered.

"You too Mike. You like a little kink with your sex?" Darcy purred.

"Who doesn't?"

"Wanna shave me?"

What is this? Some hidden camera reality show? Here's the deal, everybody has a line in the sand they won't cross. For some, watching "The Bachelorette" hoping for a glimpse of cleavage is as far as they dare go. Others go further, much further, but believe it or not, I was staring at my line in the sand.

"Oh, I don't know. I'd be afraid I might nick you or something. I'm always cutting myself and putting on the little bits of toilet paper."

Sandi handed me a razor and a can of foam. "Come on Mike, I stayed up all night listening to you bellyache, don't pussy out on me now."

As I took the razor, I began to count the piercings all over Darcy's naked bod, after I got to seven my mind was overcome with an old song: "Here's to good friends/Tonight is kinda special/The weekend comes, we'll have some fun/Tonight, tonight, let it be Lowenbrau." Knowing those kinky Germans, this was probably exactly the scene that the songwriter of that jingle had in his mind (although the song feels like an old Tony Bennett number with cheesy words, but I don't really know).

It's just past dawn. A gorgeous stripper is massaging my shoulders and licking my ear trying to convince me to shave her horny friend. What carnage would follow that is anyone's guess.

"I gotta hit the can."

"Don't be long," Darcy licked her lips.

I excused myself, walked past the bathroom and out the front door, which I closed quietly. As I crept down the steps I thought of my old friend Andy McCugh. He was the first kid to get a blow job that any of us knew. He was thirteen and he told that story like he'd traveled to some mysterious land and barely escaped with his life. I could hear his voice now, "Get back in there you wuss. There are two smokin' hot and very willing babes waiting for you. One needs a smooth, refreshing shave and who knows what the one with the rack will do to you. Turn around and get your ass back up those stairs. Seriously, you've been out all night getting drunk with a couple strippers. You went home with them for fuck's sake. If your wife caught you how much less trouble would you be in now? Might as well get your tires rotated."

I stopped on the bottom step and started to turn back. The voice of Andy had a point, what's the difference anyway? How could I let Andy and the guys down? This would be a story for the ages…and then it occurred to me I hadn't talked to Andy in fifteen years and couldn't find him now if I tried. I wasn't going to cross my line in the sand for a sex crazed, adolescent ghost. "Fuck off Andy."

September 6, 2003

This journal is turning out to be the ultimate relationship self-help book for men: "Having trouble with the missus? Go hang out with naked twenty-somethings until dawn. You too will find peace, inner happiness and your hair will reek of cigarettes. Yes, friends, it's that simple. Frequenting strip joints and drinking alcohol by the gallon is the key. Sound easy? That's because it is easy." This could be the coolest infomercial ever, don't you think?

I'm sort of regretting walking out on that threesome, but I'm trying to focus on Amaretto's, er, Sandi's advice – make amends with Alicia, make it right. Getting my mind scrambled by those scorching babes wouldn't have helped that.

After I left Sandi's I checked into the Governor Hotel and showered up. As I sit alone and write these words I realize that my tank is on empty. I pulled the autographed "O" magazine from my bag and leafed through it. I skimmed the usual makeover articles but was actually drawn in by Oprah's interview with Madonna. As I read, something caught my eye. I grabbed a pen and started at the top of the article, circling the first letter of each paragraph: "K-N-E-E-L B-E-F-O-R-E U-S P-U-N-Y M-E-N."

Kneel before us puny men. Kneel before us puny men?

Holy shit. It is Oprah. She is the stinkin' Godfather of the Stay at Home Wives Conspiracy. But she was so cool when I met her. How could she be so calculating? Then a line from the film "The Usual Suspects" hit me –

279

"the greatest deception the devil ever perpetrated was convincing the world that he didn't exist."

Mike is good people, my ass. Oprah was making me the butt of an in-joke between conspirators. How demoralizing is that?

I didn't have the heart to call Robbie and tell him he'd been right all along. Of course, Jennifer Aniston's rise as Oprah's successor was probably in the offing anyway. How is a guy like me supposed to rail against a machine like this? My buddies have deserted me – those pussies deserve the fate they get. But I know if a few of us could get together, get some momentum, strike a blow for our cause we could change things. Yeah, I do appreciate the irony of a middle aged, rich, white guy talking revolution, see how fucking upside down things are?

I know if I could tell guys everywhere what I know, what I've seen...if they could read this journal they'd know it's the truth and that could be our rallying point. Robbie has used the Internet to post some of his findings, but everything on the Internet looks like bullshit to me. I keep picturing some unshaven dude sitting in his boxers typing in made up quotes to stories. "Elvis sat right next to me on the UFO and we both impregnated the alien goddesses who had three vaginas each. As we smoked our Xeronif leaf cigarettes, the alien goddess explained to me how Rush Limbaugh's dependence on pain killers was a set up – housewives planted the drugs on him and forged those prescriptions."

Everything I read on the Internet looks loony, even CNN. And I know if somebody read this journal on the net, they'd think I was crazy as a shit house rat and I wouldn't blame them. But I could send this to Robbie and he could upload it or I could start another website. The last website I started turned out pretty good. We need some sort of mass mailing, some way of spreading the word to everyone at once, so the truth couldn't be squashed – like dropping a million copies from a B-52 bomber. But setting up a website takes time. And can I risk sending this manuscript to Robbie? What if his wife opened it first? What if the Postmaster General herself is a stay at home wife? I would need a back up plan.

In a moment of clarity, I decide to send this journal to The New York Times. Like Robert Redford in "Three Days of the Condor," I'm trying to detonate an information bomb. At this point I'm too fried to do this alone.

Here's the cover letter I wrote:

Dear New York Times Editor,

Who am I? It doesn't matter. I am just a man, a husband, a father. A man who knows things he was not meant to know. A man who has seen things he was not meant to see. A man who understands things he was not meant to understand.

What you are about to read may bend your mind. It will contradict things you have believed as true your entire life, but I swear to God in heaven that it's the truth. I will be presenting startling facts and evidence that take up where other explanations leave off. Prepare yourself. My hope is that once you understand what is really going on around you, everyday, when you have the facts about why things happen the way they do, that you will be able to fight back. Boys, we're four touchdowns behind at the two minute warning and we didn't even know we were playing a game.

I never suspected that a conspiracy of global proportions was at work, let alone at work in my own neighborhood…on my street…in my marital bed. I have been living in denial, we all have. Can I turn a blind eye? No. The monster is out of the box, it isn't going back in. I can't just sit here and ignore it, hell no. So despite the great personal risk to myself, I began a treacherous journey deep into the underground world of the stay at home wife. Deceit, propaganda and cunning met me at every turn but I felt it was my duty as an American husband, father and veteran to press on without regard to my personal safety or my sex life.

I know I am not the only man to take this journey and I want to acknowledge the brave men who fell before me. Men whose lives have become a sexless blur of "honey do" lists, chick flicks and burgers without buns. Without witnessing their pain and sacrifice I wouldn't have the courage to write the very words you are reading. I write these words with the hope that men of courage will read them and band together to salvage our own lives and, somehow, save our sons from this dark and hideous fate.

Sincerely,

A Friend

Ten minutes at the UPS Store and my journal is packaged up and ready to fly. Opting to mail it myself, I walked to a nearby postal drop and approached the mailbox feeling like the damn Unabomber. I swung the door open and dangled the package over the darkness.

"Hey Mike, whatcha doing?"

I looked up to see Kristen and Debra hanging around on the sidewalk, sipping coffee.

"Nothing," I said.

Kristen grinned, "Wild night, huh?"

"Average, I'd say."

Debra did a spit take, "Alicia will be interested to learn that two exotic dancers in one night is 'average.'"

"What are you talking about? I was alone at the Governor."

"Mike, please, who do you think you're dancing with? You didn't check in until half past six," Kristen sneered.

"What's in the package Mike?" Debra inched closer.

"Nothing. Oregon Salmon for my brother," I lied.

"Addressed to *The New York Times*?"

"He's a paperboy." Give me a break here. I was up all night.

Kristen held out her hand, "Be smart Mike."

I let go of the journal, it landed with a thud at the bottom of the mailbox.

"That was not smart Mike," Kristen shook her head.

As they walked away, Oprah's voice rang through my head, "Your life is over Mike. Your wife and her friends are going to make your life a living hell if you try and fight us. We'll turn your friends and even your children against you. And I will personally see to it that every girl you ever kissed, spanked, licked or porked will show up on my 'Oprah After the Show' on Oxygen, and we're gonna talk about your white ass and your small dick until you wish you were D-E-D, dead."

Now, I realize in real life Oprah probably wouldn't use the word 'porked' to describe sex, but that's what I heard in my head so I'm writing it here. Oprah was right about one thing, I couldn't win this fight alone. All I could do now is hunker down and wait for reinforcements.

September 9, 2003

I eased the Mercedes SUV into the Catlin Gabel parking lot and took my place behind the soccer moms driving their Hummers, Expeditions, Yukons, Suburbans, Town & Countrys, Voyagers, Volvo SUVs and BMW wagons. I sipped a double tall non fat Vanilla latte as excited children streamed from the school. Suddenly, the Mercedes rocked as the doors flew open and Andy, Timmy and Brent hit the SUV like a terrorist ambush.

"Hi Dad," shouted Andy.

"Dad, guess what? Guess what?" yelled Timmy.

Brent simply held out the first assignment of the school year, the proverbial "what I did last summer" essay, four sentences scrawled in the hand of a kid who had dinked around all summer. Across the top of the page, a bright red "E" for excellent. He smiled proudly, I kissed his forehead.

"Dad? Guess what?" Timmy persisted.

"What big guy?"

"Eric Sastaad crapped his pants during SSR," he beamed like this was the greatest thing ever accomplished by a third grader.

"SSR?" I asked.

"Sustained Silent Reading. We're supposed to be quiet but Eric crapped his pants."

Andy laughed, "Everybody in school heard about it."

"He was trying to fart during sustained silent reading cause that's when it's quiet. He kept trying to fart and trying to fart but then he crapped. He crapped his pants right at his desk," Timmy ranted. "This is the best day ever."

Does it get any better than that? No. I'm here to tell you it does not get any better. His innocence on display, all that excitement and energy over some kid trying to get a laugh and shitting himself instead, my little man will remember this day for the rest of his life. As for Eric Sastaad, he could grow up to become the greatest quarterback in the history of the NFL, but he'll always be known to these kids as the boy who tried to fart but crapped instead.

As I pulled out of the parking lot, I politely waved at Kristen, Debra, Melinda and whoever that busty red head is. These wenches were enjoying this, let me tell you. People get brave around the dog with sharp teeth once he's been neutered…and that's exactly what I want them to think.

I had crawled back home and apologized to Alicia for my erratic behavior.

I sold out and copped to the mid-life crisis and she took me back. I think I came off as sincere. She was understanding, "Lots of men suffer a mid-life crisis, it's nothing to be ashamed of," she said. I smiled a sad, knowing smile and suppressed the urge to vomit.

Either way there was no longer any question who the boss is at our house. I guess you could say an official transfer of power took place, like I had any power in the first place, right?

Adding insult to injury, I returned home to discover that my "couchless" den had been remodeled into Alicia's new workout room. Mirrors covered the walls where my sports memorabilia used to be displayed (I didn't bother to ask where the stuff went and Alicia didn't offer). The carpet was now covered with hardwoods, and the room was dwarfed by a huge Pilates machine (looks like a fucking medieval torture rack to me) and a sleek black treadmill with all sorts of screens and display panels. A rack with pastel colored free weights ran along the far wall. All that was missing was a tanned, twenty five year old personal trainer named Zach or Skip. My TV was now mounted on the ceiling over the treadmill – a Jane Fonda exercise video played on the screen. What was that, a nod to a fearless patriot or merely a sharp stick to my good eye? Talk about flogging a dead horse.

September 10, 2003

After picking up the kids from school today, I received a disturbing call from my mother. Apparently there was an incident involving Uncle Fred. Aunt Gina and Aunt Mildred were preparing to leave for Egypt, the limousine taking them to the airport was out front when Uncle Fred cried out in terrible pain – the kind of pain that can only come from watching Bernie Williams misjudge a fly ball. Aunt Gina, Aunt Mildred and the limo driver raced into the room to find Uncle Fred – on his feet – cursing at his super cool television. Turns out Darren Erstad stroked a line shot, Bernie took a step in, froze and then retreated only to watch the ball carom off the centerfield wall, two runs scored on what should've been a routine out. So Uncle Fred losing his mind was completely understandable, trouble was he'd completely blown his cover.

Ranelle ran in to see Uncle Fred throwing his wheel chair.

"You stupid fuck! We'd be better off with Darryl 'goddamn' Strawberry smoking his crack pipe in centerfield," Uncle Fred screamed.

Aunt Gina and Aunt Mildred stood there, slackjawed.

"It's a miracle!" cried Ranelle.

I guess Aunt Gina didn't buy the miracle explanation, but you got to hand it to Ranelle for trying. Turns out Gina really had no idea that Uncle Fred had been scamming her for damn near thirty years. And when she and Aunt Mildred did the math and figured out that Ranelle and Uncle Fred were more than nurse/patient, she lost her mind. Uncle Fred was going down for the count. Aunt

Gina threatened to kill him, then kill Ranelle, then, when she calmed down, she threatened to turn Uncle Fred in for insurance fraud. I can't imagine Mass Mutual would be particularly understanding, Uncle Fred has racked up one heinous medical bill.

When the smoke cleared, Ranelle was gone and Aunt Gina had checked Uncle Fred into the Alzheimer's wing at Harmony Acres Rest Home. Aunt Gina gave him an ultimatum, either keep up the ruse and lay low at the senior center or she'd turn him over to the insurance commission.

We lost another good man today, let's have a moment of silence for Uncle Fred.

September 11, 2003

Hit a bucket of balls this morning. To be honest, I'd be in less pain if I'd actually been hitting my own balls with this fairway driver.

Things are as normal around the house as they're going to be. Alicia is cheery and sweet, without a care in the world. Hortenzia, our housekeeper, has returned from Guadalajara to take over the housework, cooking and babysitting chores from Alicia, so that my wife can devote all of her time to her duties as stay at home wife conspirator.

As I diligently worked my way through today's "Honey Do" list, Uncle Fred was on my mind. I contemplated flying to New York and busting Uncle Fred out of Harmony Acres. I could call my accountant, cash in some bonds, and the two of us could party in the Virgin Islands forever. But I'd miss my kids too much, that's the master stroke of this conspiracy – the wives get us attached to the kids. They let us see ourselves in those kids and we can't turn our backs on them. Even those guys who do walk away, who crack under the pressure of the conspiracy, their souls are burned to a crisp. They'll be shuffling their feet and mumbling for the rest of their lives. The stay at home wives have laid the ultimate trap, men can't escape intact. You can never truly leave your family. In the quiet moments the men who have tried realize that there is no way out.

Stopped at Home Depot to pick up an air freshener for the Mercedes – that car has not been right since the incident with the neighbor's dog. Since I'm picking up the kids most days I've been driving the Mercedes and Alicia has been driving my Porsche…I don't want to talk about it.

Almost applied for a job at Home Depot, though. I was watching an old chubby gray haired guy helping some guy pick out wood for a fence. I imagined the old guy was a retired shop teacher who needed a little extra money, but mostly, wanted to be out in the world doing something that made him feel useful. Been a long time since I felt useful.

On the way home I drove by the Goodwill to drop off a couple boxes of clothes that my kids had out grown. I carried the boxes inside.

"Where should I put them?" I asked the heavy set woman behind the counter.

"You mind taking them out to the truck for me. Normally, I wouldn't ask you but my bunions are killing me. These dogs are barking, let me tell ya."

"Sure, it'd be my pleasure." Just to see if I could make the pain any worse I actually thought about asking her if she needed a foot rub. I don't think it would've mattered. I take two steps and a voice in my head shouts out, "Dead man walkin'."

I walked into the parking lot and up the ramp onto the Goodwill trailer truck.

"Set 'em anywhere, thanks man," said some dude in a yellow vest smoking behind the building.

I set the boxes on top of a beat up old dresser. As I turned to leave, I caught a glimpse of something out of the corner of my eye. I turned to look, half expecting the mirage to vanish, it didn't.

"My fucking couch," I cried out.

The smoking dude stuck his head around the corner, "What's up?"

"That is my fucking couch."

"Okay, man, easy. Everything here has been donated –"

"How much for my fucking couch?"

"Well, I –"

"I'll give you a hundred dollars for this fucking couch."

"I don't know if –"

I whipped out a hunny and waved it in his face.

"You were driving the Mercedes, right? Let me help you load up."

I put the Mercedes SUV into drive and took a relaxing, deep breath – the aroma tasted like a heavenly combination of Pine Sol, dog diarrhea, and musty beer couch – it smelled like freedom.

I paid cash in advance for six months at the Public Storage unit. The ten by ten unit was barely wide enough to hold the Beast. I left the roll top door up and plopped down on my couch savoring the customary plume of ancient beer odor. I cracked open a MacTarnahan's Ale, poured a little on the couch to add to my collection of beer stains and pounded the bottle.

For the first time since I discovered the Stay at Home Wives Conspiracy I felt like myself. They couldn't touch me here. This place was mine. My storage unit, my couch, my beer – if I wanted to pound this whole six pack then piss it all out in the corner there would be nothing those yentas could do about it. Public Storage unit number 12 will be my new kingdom, my haven, the world headquarters to the Circle of Trust movement. I wonder if I can get a DSL line dropped in here? Guys from everywhere could use our super secret, no girls allowed website to share their stories. We'd swap information and in time we would become as organized and united as the housewives. Yes, friends, the revolution will begin at www.thecot.net.

Being reunited with my couch had given me a little kick in the ass, a little hope. From this beer stained couch the resistance would begin. One day I'll bring my boys here, we'll tell their mother that we're going bowling or something, and I'll teach them what I've learned. They'll sit on this couch, drink a beer with their old man and I'll make them understand what they're up against, make them understand the unspeakable evil the housewives are capable of. Does that sound pathetic? Does that sound hopeless? There will be no surrender. Not ever.

I just had a thought: what are the chances that Darcy chick is still handcuffed to Amaretto's bed?

Afterword

I started out writing this book telling everyone how strange it felt writing a book when I am not a writer, but I met a guy on a plane who was a writer and he told me that if I was writing a book then I was a writer, too. I thought that was kind of cool.

After three years of trying to write this thing, I ran into a guy filming a commercial at my house and told him of my struggles. He suggested that maybe I was not a very good writer. Hey, that's not cool. My friends, that man's name was Dan Merchant and he is surely a writer, and helped me finish this book.

Thanks Dan, and by the way, my name is on the cover, too, so I guess I am a writer after all. What's up!

Dan, you did an awesome job, even if we don't sell one rotten book. Thank you, sir.

BST

• • •

This book is dedicated to my Mom, Dorothy C. Taylor. She dedicated her life to her family when my deadbeat dad left her hanging in the wind. Never complained, considered herself blessed for the little she ever had, and taught each one of us kids what it was like to have unconditional love because that's what you should get as a kid from your parents. She passed away two weeks after she retired, cancer got her. Poor woman never got a moment's peace but you never would hear that from her.

Thanks God for my Mom.
BST

Scott's Acknowledgements: *Honey, the book is not about me or any of my buddies; it is purely fictitious. I know it seems very coincidental, in fact there were times as I wrote this it got weird for me to see how much Mike was like me. Anyway, thanks for all your support and inspiration. You are a great Mom and Wife. I love you.*

To my children: Cody, Ally, Jack, Elizabeth. You are the best and make me very proud. Now go clean your stinkin' rooms.

My brother Bob and I had many interesting conversations about this stuff and he encouraged me to make it happen. Thanks Bro.

My sister Kathy thinks I'm crazy and I love her for that.

The Forest Heights crew that were always there to keep me going and laugh even before Dan made it really funny: Wade, Chris, John and Jackie, Wayne, Keno, Danny, Randy, Brandt, Fran, Tiger, Robby, High Hat, The Barnes Brothers, Ken, Foti, the TAOW crew, Kyla, Malia, Blackfish Creative, Drew, Dan.

A special thanks to all the stay-at-home wives I met, I mean that Mike met, along the way, for without their stories I would never have been so outraged to write this book in the first place.

All the other people along the way that have inspired me that now wish they did-n't because I didn't even mention their names. Damn it.

Dan's Acknowledgements: *Very Special Thanks to: Kara, Nick and Nate – my loving family, that is, thank the Lord, not at all like Mike O'Brien's.*

Special Thanks to: Scott "Maximum Chisler" Taylor, J-hole and everyone at Lightning Strikes Entertainment, John, Adrienne, Joe and all at The Gersh Agency.

So Special they get their own Thank You: The McVey Starbucks Crew: Terry, Jan, Nicole, Leslie, Stanford and all the other fabulous baristas who ever gave me a free coffee mocha while I squatted in their fine establishment during the writing of this book.

Shout Outs to: JT, Duran Duran and the Chicago House of Blues backstage crew, Roger and Pete – two real good looking boys, Susan, Rachel, Sarah, Jim and all at Warner Bros. Drama, Jim Sharp, Jeff Dujfov, Eddie Wang, Hos, Marcus, The Bosshouse Music Boys, Joe A., the incomparable Jim Melkonian Esquire, The Tragically Hip, The Magical Elves – Jane and Dan, Stephanie, Terry Currier, Mike at Darkhorse, R2 Mafia, Robert V. Gaulin, Mistii's Travel Agency, Jimmy Lambada RIP, Brightwater Ent., the Strange Frequency family and the whole "Man Down" gang, and, lastly, all of my fellow alumni of Seabeck, Twin Lakes, Lakota, North Kitsap, Curtis and PLU.